Guests of Summer

Theunis Piersma

Guests of Summer
A House Martin love story

with a foreword by Ian Newton

BTO BOOKS

Published by BTO Books, Thetford
BTO Books is the trading name of BTO Services Limited,
The Nunnery, Thetford, Norfolk, IP24 2PU

01842 750050
info@bto.org
www.bto.org
Charity Number 216652 (England & Wales), SC039193 (Scotland)

First published by Bornmeer as *Sweltsjes fan Gaast* (2014)

ISBN 978-90-858157-0

Text © Theunis Piersma

Chapter vignettes: Jos Zwarts

Printed by: Swallowtail Print

Artwork cover: Carry Akroyd

All rights reserved. No part of this publication may be reproduced, stored in a retrieval system, or transmitted in any form or by any means, electronic, mechanical, Internet, photocopying, recording or otherwise, without the prior written consent of the publishers.

Neither the publishers nor the authors can accept liability for the use of any of the materials or methods recommended in this book or for any consequences arising out of their use, nor can they be held responsible for any errors or omissions that may be found in the text or may occur at a future date as a result of changes in rules, laws or equipment.

Environment: The paper used for this book has been certified as coming from well-managed forests and other controlled sources according to the rules of the Forest Stewardship Council.

MIX
Paper from responsible sources
FSC
www.fsc.org   FSC® C015829

This book was printed and bound in Norwich by Swallowtail Print, an FSC certified company for printing books on FSC mixed paper in compliance with the chain of custody and on-product labelling standards.

CONTENTS

Foreword by Ian Newton..................................... v

Revisiting Gilbert White...................................... 1
The 'swallows' of a village.................................. 4
Shared names from history................................ 9
James Bond.. 12
The Old School... 14
The waiting game... 17
The beauty of mysteries.................................... 21
Birds of happiness.. 23
Feast of strength.. 27
Sleeping martins.. 31
Mud cottages and clay thieves......................... 34
Bedclothes... 37
Sex and violence.. 40
Cold blood... 43
Martins in infancy.. 46
Hobbies – an aerial threat................................ 50
Louse flies... 53
Malaria.. 56
Insect-eating orcas.. 59
Shakespeare and the sweet scent of dung....... 64
House Martin statistics.................................... 67

Squawking blankets over green............................ 72
Alarm at the Oxford bridges................................ 74
Countryside detectives... 78
Athletes in poverty... 84
Swifts... 86
Migration secrets revealed................................... 89
To the Congo too?... 93
Epilogue: travel companions................................ 97
Acknowledgements.. 99
Published sources of information used................ 105

FOREWORD
by Ian Newton

IT IS A PLEASURE to write a Foreword to this book by one of my favourite ornithologists. Theunis Piersma is best known internationally for his ground-breaking research on shorebirds – those birds that one sees in winter on wild and windswept coastal flats. Much as I like these birds, the very thought of their winter habitat makes me feel cold, so it came as a pleasant surprise to find him writing about the more familiar and much-loved House Martin, a charming gem of a bird closely associated with our own homes and gardens in the warmth of summer.

Reading this delightful account, one gets the impression that much of the work for the book – both the observations and the thinking – was done in the comfort of a garden chair, enjoying the sunshine, with occasional bouts of the greater activity necessary, for example, to catch and ring the adults.

In 2001, Theunis and his partner Petra decided to buy the old schoolhouse in the village of Gaast, close to where he was raised as a boy in the Frisian countryside of northern Netherlands. House Martins nested on this building (by now converted to a dwelling house) and, despite the efforts of the previous owner to deter them, they returned the following year. The new house owners did much to encourage the birds, so that their numbers built up slowly over several years, providing a source of enjoyment and observation, the results of which form the subject of this book.

This is not a text that is crammed with graphs, tables of data and statistical analyses, but a swift-moving, engaging and thought-provoking account of the lives of these birds, supported here and there by other information taken from the scientific literature. You can read the book in a few hours, but it will leave with you a warm feeling about the bird itself, a sense of knowing more about its world, and a legacy of challenging questions and ideas for the future.

The author paints a nostalgic picture of the Frisian countryside as it was in his youth. But like much of western Europe, this countryside has suffered under the impacts of modern industrialised agriculture. The wet meadows, with their breeding waders, have mostly gone, along with the colourful flowers and insects which were once a part of everyday life. All are now replaced by the monotonous green of intensively grown ryegrass and cereals. You may be surprised that the House Martins that share our homes, and hardly ever come to ground, have suffered from these landscape changes just as much as many other birds.

House Martins live on tiny aerial insects – the so-called aerial plankton – but these insects themselves depend on the habitats and wild plants that modern agriculture has largely destroyed. In Britain, the monitoring of this aerial plankton over the past few decades, by use of suction traps placed high above the ground, has revealed the fate of these tiny insects over the period of agricultural change. In general, the mass of insects caught in suction traps, as well as in other sampling programmes, has declined substantially over the years since 1970. These declines probably result mainly from the destruction of the semi-natural habitats, flowers and other food sources that once supported them. But in addition, the routine use of insecticides on farmland cannot have helped, and nor can the insect-killing anthelmintics now present in cattle-dung. In all kinds of ways, current agricultural practices have waged a ceaseless multi-fronted war against the insect world, and there is no doubt that the insects are losing.

Many people will be aware of this from a common experience mentioned in this book. Anyone of appropriate age will remember the time when cleaning insects from car windscreens was a frequent task, and an invariable consequence of a long summer journey. Nowadays one can drive for weeks at a time without ever needing to do this. This is one of the most obvious manifestations of the massive decline in insect populations which has occurred since the 1970s. Studies imply that this is largely, if not entirely, due to developments in agriculture. Like so many other birds, House Martins depend entirely on insects and the like. They are specialists. There is nothing else they can eat. Little wonder that, in the years since 1970, House Martin numbers in the Netherlands and in England are estimated to have declined by about two-thirds.

My own first memory of House Martins is not a pleasant one. I must have been about nine years old, and as I walked along our road, I noticed a rather sour-faced woman leaning out of a bedroom window with a long-handled brush, knocking down the martin nests from above the window. I took an instant dislike to her, and shed no tears when a few years later she died. But may she rest in peace, enabling future martins on that house to nest in peace. In our village in Derbyshire, few houses had the overlapping roof which seemed necessary to attract House Martins, but on those that did, the martins were usually present year after year. I remember thinking how easy it would be to count the nests, and monitor the changes in numbers from year to year. Fortunately, some people did just this in different places, and it is their counts that have allowed us to assess the extent of the recent declines.

I wondered where House Martins spent the winter, a question which has now been partly answered by modern science, as you will find in this book. I also asked my father where House Martins could have nested before people built suitable houses. He suggested cliffs as a possibility. In the many years since that time, I have only twice come across colonies of House Martins on natural cliffs (both coastal). This may reflect the extent to which these birds have taken to our homes and other buildings, and how widespread they must have become since these new nesting structures became available. In recent years, House Martins have abandoned many of their long-used buildings, reflecting their recent decline and clearly signalling that, whatever the situation in the past, they are no longer limited by shortage of potential nesting places.

Variations in the weather may affect the activity of flying insects, and hence the breeding or survival of House Martins, perhaps contributing the year-by-year ups and downs in their numbers. But these are merely annual fluctuations on a long-term downward trend for which some different explanation must be sought. In birds like the House Martin, which winter in far away lands, there is always the possibility that the agents of decline are acting there rather than here. This might be especially true for the House Martin, you might think, because we know so little about the bird in Africa, as this book confirms. But we do know for sure that they now have much less to eat in their temperate breeding areas than they had in the past. Their decline here coincided with a known decline in their food supplies, and has been more severe in places where agriculture has been most intense. This gives a strong pointer to where one problem might lie.

Wherever one dips into this book, there is interesting stuff to be found, and many of the findings provoke suggestions for further work. Although largely translated from the original Frisian, the book has been revised and adapted for the British reader, and additions of special relevance in Britain have been made. I hope you enjoy the book as much as I have.

Revisiting Gilbert White

Jacob de Groot, the boy next door, spends all of his free time scouring the agricultural fields between the villages of Gaast and Ferwâlde with his metal detector looking for old coins. On one particular afternoon he called on me as he had a strange hit in some dredge spoils – the weeds and mud removed from a ditch – a small bird ring with a number and an address: 'Vogeltrekstation Arnhem'.

Was it of any use to me, he inquired. After all, I am 'the bird man' of Gaast, a little village in the south-west of the Netherlands province of Friesland. Identifying the bird to which the ring had been attached is not a problem in the internet age: just type www.vogeltrekstation.nl and fill out the digits on the ring. The answer popped up instantly: this ring had been fixed to a House Martin two years earlier. It was captured at its mud nest on the house of Lammert and Karin Miedema, 100 metres down the road.

Did the bird's ring's final resting place in mud mean that the ancient folklore could be true after all? People all over Europe believed for a long time that House Martins and other hirundines hibernated in the mud. In the second half of the 18th century, Samuel Johnson, at that time an influential writer, lexicographer and literary critic in England, summarised this nature tale by writing: "*Swallows certainly sleep all winter. A number of them conglobulate together, by flying round and round, and then all in a heap throw themselves under water, and lye in the bed of a river.*"

Yet there were always questioning minds. Around 1220 a monk called Caesarius von Heisterbach, the Abbot of the Cistercian abbey in Königswinter in Germany, recorded an unusual story about a man who had caught a Swallow. He tied a note around the little creature's leg, which said: "*Oh Swallow, where art thou in winter?*" A year later the bird returned, carrying another note around its leg: "*In Asia, with Peter.*"

For centuries the bickering continued over where swallows and martins are when they are not with us. The Swedish natural historian Carl Linnaeus, who took his doctoral degree in Harderwijk in the Netherlands, came up with a convenient method for naming plants and animals in 1735. Back home, in Uppsala, he named the House Martin *Hirundo urbica* but in the very year that the universities of Harderwijk and Franeker (in Friesland) were closed, in 1811, others redubbed the little bird *Delichon urbicum*.

In 1757 Linnaeus presented an extensive work on bird migration, but failed to tell us whether martins and swallows migrate south before the winter, or whether they hide in mud among rocks or tree-stumps for months. He simply did not know, and left the matter open.

The German Johann Frisch took another stab at the issue. Ten years after the publication of Linnaeus' book, he tied pieces of dyed string around the legs of Swallows. Some of the birds returned the next summer with strings that had retained their watercolour pigment, which led Frisch to conclude that the birds did not spend winter in wet mud.

During that same period the French aristocrat and biologist Georges de Buffon held Swallows under water to see if they would survive… once the birds drowned, the Count was able to discount the mud story.

Also in that epoch, the Reverend Gilbert White of Selborne in Hampshire, a keen observer who seemed more preoccupied with the study of nature than with the salvation of his parishioners, could not imagine that House Martins would winter very far from his English village. While I think he was much too capable an interpretive ornithologist to believe in hibernation in mud, White did launch an investigation. On 11 April 1781, the last date before he had ever seen House Martins return to the village, White *"employed some men to explore the shrubs and cavities of the suspected spot. The persons took pains, but without any success."* As they were doing their search for 'slumbering' House Martins, they noticed one flying over Selborne, briefly visiting an old mud nest.

Fifty years later, yet another Swede named Samuel Ödmann argued that it was impossible for hirundines to hibernate in the mud because they often turned up in Sweden well before the ice on ponds started to melt. Ödmann could not imagine Swallows breaking through a thick layer of ice.

In 1854, the Swedish Scientific Academy declared that in Stockholm they had reached a conclusion. The controversy over the location of hibernation was resolved. Whatever the ring issued by the Dutch Vogeltrekstation and found by Jacob de Groot seemed to suggest: House Martins do not hibernate in the mud.

OK, but where do they go?

The 'swallows' of a village

It is mid-April, and like a headless chicken I reel around the house. I gaze at the sky: the House Martins should have arrived days ago. As the news about stock markets dictates the rhythm of some people, so the comings and goings of migratory birds are important to me. There is always that latent fear that one spring the birds will not return, that the world is in such turmoil that the artful aviators will no longer be capable of completing their passage to Europe.

Of course the same concerns relate to the Black-tailed Godwits, Knots, Ruffs and Spoonbills that I study during my day job, but most of all they are about the swallow-like birds which share my home village. They come in four kinds. Look up on a summer day, and high above a village or a town you will see sickle-shaped birds sail and hunt and skim: Common Swifts. The fact that Swifts are so similar to swallows is due to the similarities in life style: their behaviour in the air and a diet consisting of little flies and aphids.

At lower elevations and more likely over villages than over towns we see swallow-like birds with much shorter flight movements, dancing and sliding with occasional wing beats, circling: white-rumped, dark-backed House Martins. Flying nearer to the ground than House Martins we can find Sand Martins. They have the build of a House Martin, but they are dark brown on top and a lighter grey underneath, and they come without a white rump. Once I was lucky enough to hold a Sand

Martin in my hands. It struck me how closely their streamlined head resembles that of the Swift: a grey face with large forward-looking black eyes and with heavy brows.

To spot the fourth swallow species, the Barn Swallow with its long and elegant forked tail and rusty-red breast, one must not look up but down instead. Barn Swallows buzz copses and ditches, hunting for flies. These birds are a bit larger than both martins but not as big as Common Swifts.

Swifts do not build nests themselves; they breed under a tile or in some other elevated cavity underneath a sloping roof. Sand Martins dig a small hole in a steep sandy bank, while House Martins shape from mud a rounded nest under a roof-gutter or gable of a house. Barn Swallows do the same, but they often choose a location under a roof, preferably inside a barn which is swarming with flies. Usually they stick their nest to an inside wall, or a timber beam, a short distance below the roof, but not touching it. They do not build a roof for their clay nest, leaving it as an open cup.

The cup of Barn Swallows is similar to, or even smaller than that of House Martins, so relative to their body size it is rather small. This becomes evident when the young Barn Swallows get fully feathered and clearly need all the space above and around the cup to move. Quite clearly, in foul weather they need the protection of a building or a cave. House Martins don't, they do all their stuff inside their house of clay and can afford outdoor locations.

Carl Linnaeus believed that the four species were blood relatives, but now it has been established that swifts are of a completely different order than the 'hirundine' trio. Interestingly swifts are related to hummingbirds and owls, and have long history as the first versions flew around in the dinosaur era. The real swallows, the family of birds called Hirundinidae, did not emerge until 20 million years later – dinosaurs had become extinct by then. Yet, the emergence of true swallows still happened a mighty 50 million years ago; they have been on Earth ten times as long as human beings!

I love all four of them, but House Martins, in particular, fascinate me. Although they are widespread throughout Europe, there is so little we really know about them. We know something about their numbers, a little about their diet, but hardly anything about their social life. We know next to nothing about the time that they are not with us. Well over a million have been ringed, but very few have been recovered in winter, all in Africa.

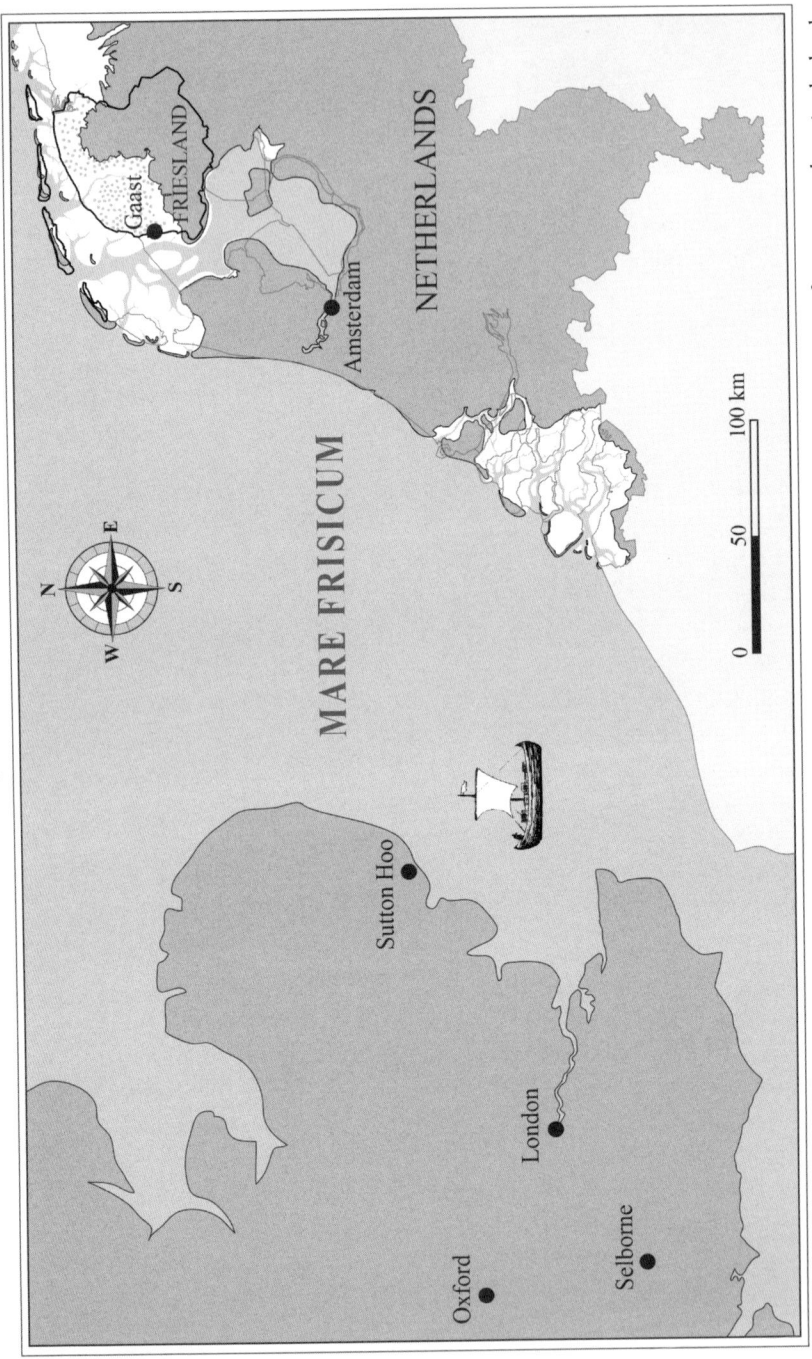

Map of the southern North Sea and the lands directly west and east of it in the period 600–800 AD. The names of important places in the book are indicated, and show that the village Gaast, now protected by a seawall on the Dutch mainland, was situated on a vast saltmarsh dotted with man-made elevations ('terpen') on which the Anglo-Frisians of the time lived, and from where they journeyed by boat to and from their freshly settled brethren in East Anglia. Map by Dick Visser.

Shared names from history

In mid-August 2014 I paid a visit to Sutton Hoo, the hamlet on the east side of the River Deben in Suffolk that is now a major tourist attraction, owned and managed by the National Trust. Here you can see a series of man-made mounds from the sixth and seventh centuries AD that have yielded many archaeological treasures. The mounds contained the graves of what must have been VIPs, including a burial in a ship of a man regarded as the first truly Anglo-Saxon king, King Rædwald. He died in AD 624 or 625.

Opening Sutton Hoo's 'souvenir guide', I immediately encounter a drawing of a small group of Anglo-Saxon women chatting and otherwise going about their business on the shore of the river, sometime around AD 600. The drawing shows a small flock of Barn Swallows flying over their heads, just as they do over mine when I examine the picture! What the brochure does not tell readers is that we actually know what the women called these birds at the time: swealve.

These were the days, some 1,400 or 1,500 years ago, when the forerunners of the English and Frisian languages hardly differed, if at all. The contemporary Frisian word for swallow – swel or sweltsje – derives from swealve. The word means 'swiftly moving': rapidly flying. Swealve sprang from an even older Germanic word with the same meaning: swalvon. This word was thus the cradle of svala (Swedish), swallow (English), and sualow (Scots).

In England, House Martins have become locally known under many different names that include Eave Swallow, House Swallow, Martin Swallow, Martinet, Martlet, Meadow Martin, White-rumped Swallow, Window Martin and Window Swallow. Whenever I speak or write Frisian, I may use the words sweltjes, swellen or hússwellen as alternatives. However, I would have preferred to call them thússwellen or Home Swallows, because they are the swallows of my home, my heart.

Just as Barn Swallows and House Martins share ancestors, so do the English and the Frisians. These are the two languages, and the two people, that originate from members of a Germanic tribe who started moving west after the fall of the Roman Empire, from c AD 400. The people on the move were farmers as well as seafarers, and may have included people coming from southern Scandinavia or northern Germany.

They chose the 'terpen', the earthen mounds made on the Wadden Sea saltmarshes, to escape the highest tides and settled among what may have been left of the earlier Frisian folk known by the Romans. They also moved across the southern North Sea to live next to, and among, the Britons of Gaelic descent that then still lived a Roman culture. On both sides of the sea the newcomers became a dominating social force, and in the course of the development of their connected patchwork of small kingdoms (AD 500–700), they successfully left their language, their culture and their genes. Over half of English men, and close to 100% of the Englishmen from East Anglia, carry a recognisable Frisian variant of the DNA on the Y-chromosome.

The grave at Sutton Hoo, which could well have housed King Rædwald, contained the remains of a 27-metre-long and four-metre-wide wooden ship richly endowed with remarkable goods and jewellery, including a silver helmet shaped around the image of a Shoveler, with the Shoveler's tail representing the helmet's moustache, the body of the duck its nose, the wings forming a pair of eye brows, and the head and bill being a decorative ridge on the helmet's 'forehead'.

The majestic coffin that was built from a well-used ship might well have symbolised the importance and magnitude of the marine exchanges at the time, the connections between what was becoming England and what soon would be called Frisia again. The Anglo-Frisians will have traded products of the farming grounds on the mainland saltmarshes. The amazingly sophisticated ornaments from this time found in both Friesland and Suffolk are evidence of advanced forms of craftsmanship.

Eventually, the distinct historical contexts on either side of Mare Frisicum (the name given to the southern part of the North Sea) led to a divergence in the fastest-changing characteristics of people: their culture and language (rather than their genes). Whereas King Rædwald dabbled with Christianity (he was said to maintain two altars, one for the new God and one for the old pagan gods), his later nephews in Frisia like King Aldgisl and King Rædbad still fought for their original beliefs. The mainland Anglo-Frisians lost their spiritual and narrative culture to the Christian forces about 200 years after the English Anglo-Frisians lost theirs. One can speculate that this earlier shift to Christianity in England led to a widening of the cultural gap across Mare Frisicum.

What about the swallows and martins during these early Middle Ages? On the Frisian mainland the early Anglo-Frisians lived in large houses built of earth sods, and it is hard to imagine House Martins building mud nests on their grassy eaves. It is easier to imagine Barn Swallows building nests on the supporting beams inside the farmhouses, though cooking smoke might have deterred them. It is thought that the original habitat of Barn Swallows was in caves, a habitat unknown in the Anglo-Frisian territory at the time. House Martins would still be limited to nesting on bare cliffs, as they have done in some places in Britain even recently.

James Bond

When the name James Bond is mentioned, I automatically think of Sean Connery, my favourite actor in the role of this fictional figure created by the English novelist Ian Fleming, but there was another Bond connected to the world of ornithology. Fleming was a bird-lover and while watching birds in Jamaica he always had his *Birds of the West Indies* close at hand. The book was authored by James Bond, an ornithology professor from Philadelphia, USA, so when Fleming was looking for a short, masculine name for his English hero: 'James Bond' was spot-on. The actual James Bond had no objections – 'Fine with me,' he wrote back when he was asked and later he and his wife went birdwatching with the Flemings in Jamaica.

What connection is there between the real James Bond and our swallows and martins? Well, during World War II, he and the German-American ornithologist Ernst Mayr wrote a scientific paper in which they attempted to neatly classify all known hirundines according to the principles laid out by Linnaeus. With more than 80 swallow and martin species, the classification at the time was a bit of a shambles.

Mayr and Bond dealt with it cunningly: they took into account not only the birds' shapes and sizes, but made their nesting habit the foremost criterion. Sand Martins, for instance, dig the nests themselves, while Barn Swallows and House Martins mould their nests from clay. Particularly in the Americas one finds another brand of swallow-likes that inhabits tree cavities, often carved by woodpeckers. Like the Great Tit and the Blue Tit in our part of the world, such species may nowadays often nest in man-made nest boxes.

Mayr and Bond assumed that those swallow species which utilise the labour of others and avoid digging or moulding their own nests must be the most primitive and ancient species. From what were to become the nest-box breeders, the diggers and moulders would have evolved. Recently, using various advanced genetic techniques, biologists repeated their work. Although they confirmed that swallows with identical nest characteristics were the most closely related, the diggers, such as our Sand Martins, turned out as the most ancient. The analyses clearly showed that the evolution of swallows had started in Africa. The hirundines, therefore, are an African creation, just like hominids!

The Central and South American part of the family branched off and started nesting in cavities, either naturally existing ones or those formed by previous excavators. Mayr and Bond argued that in a humid tropical climate clay nests would too easily collapse.

Clay builders, such as our European swallows and martins, tend to settle for places where wet clay is available, but where the mud can easily dry. These clay moulders include three types: one that stops moulding once the open bowl is ready, such as the Barn Swallow; one that carries on building until the roof is on, only allowing for a tiny entrance – the House Martin; and other species that go on to construct an entry funnel. It turned out that the bigger and more complex the nest, the more recently did the species evolve. Barn Swallows have been around longer than House Martins.

The Old School

One April day in 2001 on our way to our home on the island of Texel, my partner Petra and I ran into a traffic-jam when trying to cross the 'Afsluitdijk', the 35-kilometre dam that created the large lake, Lake IJsselmeer, from the old Zuiderzee. It now separates the freshwater of IJsselmeer from the seawater of the Wadden Sea. On such occasions we tend to divert southward along the coast for a spontaneous visit to Gaast. Will there be birds in the shallow waters by the dyke, or on the unsurpassed Workumerwaard, that original piece of intertidal sandflat that is now largely extensively managed for meadow birds?

Of course we are in luck; one can hardly go wrong here. Some 7,000 Ruffs skim over the original Zuiderzee dyke, moving from what was once an intertidal sandflat and is now rough grazing and hay meadows, to the more intensively used fields around Ferwâlde, sister village of Gaast. Such a large number of Ruffs in one flock – what a unique sight! At the turn of the millennium tens of thousands could still be spotted along the Frisian IJsselmeer coast during springtime, birds that were on their way from West Africa to tundra breeding grounds in northern Europe and Asia.

We had been tempted before, but these 7,000 Ruffs managed to intensify our desire to leave Texel and move here to live, but back in 2001 there was hardly anything up for sale, let alone in tiny Gaast.

We commissioned a real-estate agent in nearby Workum to search the coastal region for us, and that summer we also rummaged through the village ourselves. In the centre of it, hidden behind a green wall of conifers, stood the old primary school. And what really struck us was the large number of House Martins nesting on the building.

Later in the year the property, which had not been in use as a school for a decade, came up for sale, so as autumn broke we went for it as potential buyers. To increase its saleability, its owner had briskly removed the martin nests after the summer. He was well aware that House Martins dislike dark colours, so he had painted the eaves green. This was a miscalculation on his part. With us as potential buyers, he could have struck a better deal without his efforts at nest removal…

By the end of March 2002, even before the property was transferred – with the owner's permission and under the watchful eyes of curious neighbours – Petra and I stood on a long ladder to turn the green eaves white again. That first spring we saw the first House Martins arrive; by the end of May the first nest on the east wall was under construction and another was started on a wall facing north. Upon our return from abroad in early July, we found three inhabited nests on the house: two on the north wall and one on the east. Compared with the tens of nests that had been removed, numbers seemed small. Perhaps the House Martins missed the attractions of old nests and the muddy traces of destroyed nests.

Three House Martin couples – it did not quite satisfy me. I discussed the matter with various colleagues and soon I met a true hirundine expert, David Winkler ('Wink') who lives in upstate New York. Over there it is quite common for the cavity-nesting Tree Swallow to breed in nest boxes, so to encourage our House Martins he suggested installing an entire row of artificial nests, lower on the wall than where martins naturally have their clay nests. This would make it easier and less dangerous for us to access. Once while checking on his own Tree Swallow boxes, Wink had taken a fall and remained in a coma for three weeks, so it was a lesson to absorb.

Petra and I were renovating anyway, so a man-made nest box constellation was not a problem. From Germany we ordered 42 artificial House Martin nests made out of wood-fibre and concrete. Carpenters built a fine timber frame onto which the nest boxes were secured. All in all it looked rather good, an 'eyebrow' on the east wall of our house.

In the subsequent summer six House Martin couples bred on the house in self-made clay nests, but none of the artificial nests was used. In 2004 the number of new nests doubled to 12, but all ignored the artificial boxes. The following year there were 18 pairs on the house and, believe it or not, just one used an artificial nest, but in 2006 the situation improved considerably. Six of the artificial nests were taken by breeding House Martins and 22 couples built their own nests. In the years to follow our colony increased even more, with 2014 setting the record with a total of 44 breeding couples. However, over the years never more than six artificial nests have been occupied so, clearly, moulding its own nest of clay must be part of a House Martin's innermost being.

The waiting game

Late in April 2008 I had a chance meeting with fellow villager Ruurdtsje de Boer who told me she'd spotted the first House Martin of the spring the day before. A year earlier we had visited her house to trap some of the martins breeding in clay nests there. While we were busy, Ruurdtsje asked where these House Martins hung out when they were absent from Gaast. It surprised her that we believed that House Martins would move all the way to Africa, but that we didn't know for sure.

The next day a note in our letter box contained Ruurdtsje's first-of-the-year House Martin sightings since 2003. My heart leapt: a soul mate in my little village! Just like me, she had the habit of jotting notes in a booklet, recording when the martins return to Gaast. Since that day a card is dropped in our letter box each year, soon after she has spotted her first bird of the new season. Here's how our records compare:

Year	Ruurdtsje	Petra and me
2003	April 23	April 16
2004	April 16	April 19
2005	April 19	April 17
2006	April 20	April 15
2007	April 6	April 13
2008	April 20	March 31

2009	April 10	April 12
2010	March 30	April 12
2011	April 14	April 3
2012	April 11	April 7
2013	April 22	April 14
2014	April 13	April 13

Though Petra and I recorded our first two House Martins on 31 March in 2008, it took until 17 April before we saw the next one and Ruurdtsje had to wait until 20 April. In 2010 Ruurdtsje was first with a House Martin seen on 30 March: the earliest bird ever. A few days later another note landed in our letter box, because she spotted the second and the third House Martins on 4 April. At the Old School we had to be patient for another week and a half, with the first appearing on 12 April.

The fact that we often noticed the first House Martins a few days before Ruurdtsje may be easily explained by Petra's hawk-eyes, and perhaps also by the number of nests on the walls of our respective houses. We have had more nests than Ruurdtsje and, as we will discover later on, the higher the number of old nests, the bigger the chance of martins returning very early in the season.

In Gilbert White's late 18th-century England, the House Martins returned on average by 16 April, with the earliest returnees arriving alone. Several weeks may elapse before large numbers return, usually by the end of April, when the trees and shrubs are budding and the woods are flushed in sap-green. For a couple of days the House Martins bounce to and fro, up and down to the old clay nests; they sit inside gibber-jabbering, or hang on remaining clay ridges. Over and over they take stock of the amount of overwinter damage, until the real work begins. This work consists of bringing new clay in order to repair old dwellings, or to build new ones. On average, I observed the first claying on 28 April, but there were years in which it started earlier (22 April in 2009) or later (5 May in 2010).

May appears to be the preferred month to build a clay nest. If a hole appears in a nest later, and is not too large, the House Martins will patch it up. Generally they won't undertake any new housing development after 5 June, except in extremely late springs. The last instances when I observed House Martins on our school working on new nest constructions have varied between 8 June (in 2008) and 18 June (in 2010), with 12 June as an average. By that time, in the earliest nests the chicks will have hatched; the first show their little beaks between 30 May (2008) and 12 June (in 2003, 2005 and 2010).

Of course there are some remarkable exceptions to the norm: at the end of July 2004 a new nest was still under construction. It was ready on 8 August and in late August some chicks were seen, although I don't believe any actually fledged. In 2013 the spring remained cold for a long time, so everything was extremely late, and the last nest began to be built as late as 4 July. It was worked on for two weeks but never finished.

I am not completely sure, but have a sense that from mid-June onwards some House Martins may already be ready to leave on their southern migration. No doubt these are birds that weren't able to start the construction of their nests on time, perhaps because they arrived late, or because they failed to chat up a mate. Or perhaps these are the House Martins that saw their dreams about sex, love, and conventional happiness shattered by too many rainy, cold days just when they should have been claying a nest. Such birds hang around until early summer, and leave in the hope of giving it a try the next year.

In the course of summer the number of House Martins over the village increases; by the last week of June the young ones from the first brood start flying. These youngsters may stay around for quite some time. In late July and early August some nests still show a lot of activity because some adults have started second broods. This can take weeks. In some years it finishes around mid-August (in 2005), but in most years it lasts until mid-September. In 2009 I saw a food-begging chick hanging from a nest on 2 October.

House Martin migration starts in earnest in August with large groups high in the air heading south and in Gaast numbers soon begin to decline. In July they can be seen flying over the village by the hundreds but, come August, it is more often by the dozen. September could be called the month of 'roof-sitting'. On sunny afternoons, tens or hundreds of House Martins, often joined by some Barn Swallows and Sand Martins, will gather to sit on sloping roofs. They chatter, they expose their backs to the sun, and they preen. I have seen this in Gaast as well as the small buildings that make up the University of Groningen field station on the Wadden Sea island Schiermonnikoog. Ian Newton often saw it as a boy in New Whittington, Derbyshire.

And an elderly Daniel Defoe, three years after publishing *Robinson Crusoe*, noticed it in Suffolk, on the Southwold church, in early October 1722: "*I observed in the evening an unusual multitude of birds sitting on the leads of the church; curiosity led me to go nearer to see what they were, and I found they were all swallows; that there was such an infinite number that they covered the whole roof of the church, and of several houses near, and perhaps might, of more houses which I did not see… this is the season of the year when the swallows, their food here failing, begin to leave us, and return to the country, wherever it be, from whence I suppose they came; and this being the nearest to the coast of Holland, they come here to embark.*"

These days, even in Holland, by early October there are no more martins to be seen. In most years it is all over by the end of September or by early October, but on 29 October 2005 there was still a single House Martin flying over Gaast. I must ask Ruurdtsje if she takes notes of her last House Martin sightings too.

The beauty of mysteries

What probably attracts me most about House Martins, apart from their physical beauty, are the mysteries that surround them. The European population runs into the millions, so they are all around us and yet we know so little about them.

From the moment I started studying House Martins in Gaast, I thought about writing this account. I intended to move fast, afraid that my knowledge of this little bird might smother me. Twelve years have passed so now I do know a lot more, but has that extra knowledge eroded the mysteries and dissolved the magic? Not as far as I'm concerned. At most, a mature, richer story is more difficult to tell. Even if we unravel the mystery of where House Martins go in winter, surely a new riddle will emerge, and our thoughts can start running wild again. Knowledge is like a balloon that keeps expanding. The bigger it gets, the larger the interface with the unknown.

While slumped in a chair in the garden with House Martins doing their aerial dances overhead, my thoughts move freely. How does the world of hirundines function? The hibernation question is one thing, but where do they sleep before they have built a nest? Where do these birds actually mate? Do young and old ones return to the same spot year after year? And what do they eat – is their diet dependent on time of year and weather?

At the start of my research I had to ask myself which questions I wanted to answer myself, taking into account the time involved. To find out about their diet, one can gather droppings and scrutinise the excrement under a microscope. Learning to identify the arthropod remains will not be easy. And it is donkey work too. Another practical question relates to disturbance; how often is one prepared to pester the birds? To determine the precise numbers of eggs and chicks, their timing and growth, one must frequently look inside a nest. This might cause stress for parents and young alike. Am I willing to go that far?

I cautiously started working with House Martins on our house and in the rest of the village from 2003 onward, step by tiny step. This book tells of these steps, but also of everything I learned about martins and swallows by reading and speaking with others about them.

Birds of happiness

"*Perhaps I can still see the swallows arrive*", the Frisian clog maker, fierljepper, and bird-lover Eelke Scherjon had remarked that winter but he passed away in early February 2012, aged 56: much younger than those around him would have wished. To Eelke, swallows and summer were inseparable. One swallow does not make a summer, but would a summer without hirundines still be a summer?

It is not so hard to imagine how things used to be in our neck of the woods. The longing for the endless, cold winter to come to a close at a time of year in which the days only just start to lengthen. The finding – and eating – of the first Lapwing eggs. The prospect of light, warmth, new life, fresh vegetables and fruits. There hardly are more obvious fine-weather birds than House Martins, Barn Swallows and Swifts. I daresay that ever since people inhabited our latitudes, swallow-like birds must have symbolised the promise of summer.

From the ancient times of the Egyptians, the Greeks and the Romans, drawings and stories about swallows have survived. The winters of the Mediterranean are hardly as long and cold as ours, yet from Hellenic times paintings exist of half-naked men, excitedly looking and pointing at a swallow up in the sky. Some 2,000 to 3,000 years ago, the Greeks and Romans were impressed by the inherently creative structure of the clay nests made by swallows and House Martins. During the times of the

Pharaohs it was even believed that swallows symbolised the connection between the stars and the souls of the dead. Whoever killed a swallow or a martin, whether deliberately or not, risked execution.

As opposed to their holy status with the Egyptians, swallows were merely regarded as omens by the Greeks and Romans – as they are with us. As early as 350 BC, the Greek natural philosopher Aristotle remarked that 'one swallow does not a summer make', an expression later popularised by William Shakespeare. Of course this is literally so, because it can become bitterly cold after the first sighting of a swallow – but also metaphorically.

Aristotle would have known the saying from one of the fables of Aesop, a poet who lived three centuries earlier. The fable tells of a young man who spends all his money drinking, eating and gambling. At some stage he owns nothing but a coat to protect himself from the winter chill. When he spots a very early swallow, he thinks: spring has arrived! He sells his coat so he can take another gamble. Perhaps he will finally make his fortune. However, he loses his last penny and then the frost sets in again. When the man finds a frozen swallow he accuses it of fraud before freezing to death himself.

It is a tale designed to teach us that we shouldn't trust ourselves too easily to be on top of things.

In the meantime, all over Europe Barn Swallows and House Martins were and are seen as messengers of prosperity. By the end of winter, farmers leave the doors of their outbuildings ajar to allow Barn Swallows to nest inside. In Germany it was said that nests of swallows and martins attached to a house or a farm would protect the building against fire. Dutch sayings like 'swallows on the roof, money in the pocket' and 'Where swallows nest no calf will die' led to warnings such as 'If you rob a swallow, your best cow will die at home.'

Interviewing the then 29-year-old ploughman Derek Warren from Suffolk, writer Ronald Blythe quoted him saying in the mid-1960s: "… *there were always the martins. Each house seems to have so many people in it and so many martins. You must never bang their mud nests down or* make them unwelcome, it is very unlucky. It is thought poor manners to destroy a martin's nest while he is abroad." In Suffolk as much as elsewhere, martins and swallows have been protected by taboos on disrupting nests long, far and wide.

For good fables we don't necessarily need to go back to Aesop's ancient Greece. In 1973 a fabulous folk tale about swallows that were fooled by a frog was told to the Frisian author Ype Poortinga by the skipper's son and fisherman Stef de Bruin. In 1976 the story was published in *The Ring of Light. Frisian Folk Tales*. The swallows in this tale must have been Barn Swallows (or perhaps Sand Martins), as they hunt for flies over water more often than House Martins do.

Why Swallows forage over water

There once was a Swallow that buzzed around over a canal, hunting for flies. He saw a frog on a water-lily leaf that was also catching flies, but without moving a muscle. Occasionally he just popped out his tongue to grab a fly. The Swallow started laughing and sneered at the frog that it was stupid, because that way he hardly caught any flies; he, the Swallow, was much quicker, and managed to catch many more flies with less effort. The frog told the Swallow not to brag about his speed, because if push came to shove, he himself would be able to swim faster underwater than the Swallow could fly through the air. Then the Swallow challenged him to prove it. A canal ran along a wood fringe, and they both agreed to start off at one end, either fly or swim as fast as they could to the other end, turn around immediately, and whoever managed to return to the starting point first was the winner. Because they were in need of some kind of control, they asked a family of Jays to act as referees. At the start, and the turning point, a Jay was posted, and three other Jays positioned themselves well apart from one another alongside the canal. They arranged for the frog to swim along the bottom of the canal, and for the Swallow to fly above it. At the checkpoints where the Jays sat the Swallow would have to call out to the frog, in response to which the frog had to pop its head out of the water. The agreement was that the loser would have to supply the winner with as many flies as he could eat in one day, every day.

The Jay at the start was to signal the beginning of the race. He sounded the starting call and off they went. The moment the Swallow reached the second Jay, he called out for the frog. It popped its head out of the water and responded. And the race continued. But it was rather odd: the frog reached each and every checkpoint where a Jay sat a fraction earlier than the Swallow, and popped its head out of the water. When the Swallow approached the mark, he called out for the frog before reaching the finish-line – and the frog popped its head out of the water before the Swallow crossed it. So the frog had won. All were taken by surprise.

But what the Swallow didn't know, nor did the Jays, was that the cunning frog had plotted with his family, and at each checkpoint where a Jay sat on the bank of the ditch, a frog sat at the bottom, ready to pop its head out of the water and answer the Swallow. Our friend had simply dived under at the start, and as the Swallow returned, he sat there already waiting. He hadn't moved an inch.

Nevertheless, this is why we still see the Swallows catching flies over water while frogs sit with their mouths open. The Swallow has to keep dropping flies in the frog's mouth until it is full up.

Feast of strength

Despite the reservations of some family members that biologists were woolly-minded butterfly catchers, I always wanted to follow that profession. Both my grandfathers were tenant dairy farmers; my father was a vet in the Frisian village of Himmelum, only about 20 kilometres from Gaast (I have not dispersed far!), so I grew up among cats, sheep and horses and my maternal grandmother, and perhaps my mother, carried some of the investigative spirit of research biologists. My grandmother definitely was adventurous, though she never actually managed to travel in her life. In her later years she regretted the fact that, despite graduating in biology, her grandson had remained so ignorant about botany.

My urge to tell stories about people and the world around us owes a lot to the inspiration of two teachers at the Protestant primary school in Bakhuzen, which experimented with the use of Frisian as the language of instruction during the first two years. I don't remember much of these years, except the reading of books on explorers such as Roald Amundsen, but in the third and fourth years Dick Eisma (1941–2011) was our teacher. Mr Eisma crossed my path again 30 years later, when he proof-read the book on Golden Plovers and the folks who catch them.

The headmaster then was Hendrik Twerda (1904–1984). I was lucky to be in his class during his last year as a school teacher, because Mr Twerda was a true scholar of local customs and folklore, and a born storyteller. When I now read his history book *Fan Fryslâns ferline* (*Of Friesland's Past*), I still hear his voice. In his last year of teaching, Mr Twerda ordered a blackout of the classroom once or twice a week.

Suddenly he would say: "*Andries! Pegs on the curtains and wall charts in front of the windows.*" As quickly as possible, Andries from year six would put up the big geographic wall charts to cover the windows facing the corridor and the other classrooms, close the heavy curtains, and fix them with two pegs. Very quickly, for that was Twerda's way.

In the darkened classroom we were treated to a story. It always came with a slide show, and the black-rimmed transparencies seemed old-fashioned even then. These stories were about Frisian history, and regional folklore in particular. Mr Twerda's collection of slides was the representation of a fantastic archive of newspaper cuttings (the local Frisian newspaper, the *Leeuwarder Courant*, had not yet gone online). There and then I must have developed the urge to collect newspaper cuttings – although my father had the same tendency.

My dearest memories are related to a sketching excursion to the Holle Wei (Hollow Way), an entrenched sandy path, leading from the village of Bakhuzen over a loamy clay ridge to the even smaller village of Mirns. On a hot summer's day we ventured out with our sketchbooks to draw nature and I can still visualise all those flowers, the beetles and wasps and other insects in and on the sandy shoulders of this ancient pathway. A couple of years later this would all be demolished, as the ridge became the site of Bakhuzen's new housing estate.

By the end of the 1970s I started to read biology in Groningen. There were many specialisations to choose from but I knew from the start what direction I would take: something to do with the sea, and of course with animals. I sought to join Rudi Drent's group of animal ecologists and, as soon as my biology study programme allowed it, I visited as many animal ecology lectures as possible.

One day a guest speaker from Scotland was announced. David Bryant, who came to discuss his research on House Martins, was actually English and carrying out scientific measurements that were unique at the time. Naturally, as young students we were mesmerised by this man.

He caught House Martins at his study site in Scotland where they nested under the eaves of old farm houses. These nests were not that high up, so he didn't even have to climb a ladder. He injected the birds he caught with a special type of water, released them, and caught them once again the next day. This water ($^2H_2{}^{18}O$) was so-called 'heavy water'. 'Heavy' because the hydrogen atoms (^2H) as well as the oxygen atoms (^{18}O) were of the 'heavy' variety. Please, don't stop reading here, for it soon will be fun again. Or at least more simple!

The great thing about heavy water is that, the harder the House Martins labour between the two captures, and the more energy they use, the quicker they run out of heavy water. This is caused by the fact that the oxygen disappears as carbon dioxide (CO_2) and water, and the hydrogen only as water. By taking a small blood sample during the first and the second catch, and by measuring the concentration of heavy water in those drops of blood – and performing calculations based on those findings – Bryant could tell exactly how much energy his House Martins had used.

Remember the fairy-tale that describes hirundines as eager beavers? Perhaps this is correct because, according to Bryant's measurements, House Martin parents caring for chicks work just as hard as Scandinavian lumberjacks, taking into account the animal's weight. In tests, the lumberjacks drank a set amount of heavy water, and the next day they urinated in a tube, enabling scientists to perform similar measurements and calculations to those Bryant had carried out with the House Martins. Working like lumberjacks – one wouldn't easily think that when watching House Martins skipping through the sky.

Klaas Westerterp, who was in the audience in that lecture hall, had worked with David Bryant and at the time he was setting up a heavy-water measuring system in Groningen to determine how hard owls, falcons and geese laboured – these were all birds that were in the spotlight at the time.

Later on, Westerterp moved between universities, from Groningen to Maastricht, where he became famous for measuring human energy consumption. He was particularly interested in heavy-water experiments with people who were motivated to keep their physical performance close to a maximum, such as the racing cyclists in the Tour de France who have to work very hard for a full three weeks and have an energy output rate that is similar to that of lumberjacks.

Over time more and more research has been carried out on a constantly increasing variety of species. Gradually we have come to understand that humans as well as other animals cannot, or at least will not, perform any better than the cyclists in the Tour de France, or than Bryant's House Martins. At a performance level that is four or five times higher than the energy cycle when relaxed, our body says: 'Stop! This is enough!'

Sleeping martins

To find out what energy is expended when a House Martin forages to feed its young, a comparison must be made with the bird's output during periods of sleep. But where do House Martins actually do this?

One early morning (now almost a century ago), in what I guess was a Sunday in June, the famous biologist Julian Huxley went out to watch the activities of House Martins at a breeding colony under the eaves of a little inn in Oxfordshire where he was staying. To his surprise no martins were to be seen at first light. Then a Barn Swallow left a barn, and when he followed it flying steeply up into the sky he discovered House Martins. High in the blue sky, and only just identifiable, they circled in the company of Swifts.

Before the sun rose, the birds flew lower, twittering all the time. Huxley interpreted these observations as 'sun-greeting'; he suggested that the martins left their nest in darkness and flew up to great heights to greet the sun. But 'how far above the earth they flew before they reached the light and began to circle in it and sink with it', he did not know. However, rather than them being nesting birds, could Huxley have witnessed the descent of pre-breeding martins that had spent the nights aloft – do House Martins, as well as Swifts, sleep in the air?

In spring, as soon as the first House Martins return to Gaast, they occupy the old clay nests that have come through winter undamaged.

Normally their numbers are small. At the Old School we have nests on both the east and the north walls. For some reason the nests facing north stand a better chance of surviving the winter – 70% of a sample of 67 nests remained intact there, compared with only 13% out of 131 nests facing east. Not surprisingly, then, the martins that are first to return in spring immediately dive into the north-facing nests. These birds always have a head start over the birds on the east wall.

As soon as more than 90% of the nests have been completed – that is, when the hole in the cup of clay starts to look like a proper, narrow, entrance – I was able to observe that House Martins stay the night in their nest. If the nest is only half finished, the House Martin will roost there until nightfall, but will eventually take off in the twilight. Do the observations of Huxley suggest where House Martins without completed nests sleep?

If House Martins were like Barn Swallows or Sand Martins, they would roost in the reed beds outside the village for the night – just like the hundreds, or thousands, or tens of thousands of Starlings which disappear into the reeds at Gaast at winter dusk. Barn Swallows and Sand Martins are accustomed to sleeping in reed beds, as it is this habitat – or where reeds are lacking, sturdy grass – that they often choose when in their African winter quarters. Dutch ornithologists Rob Bijlsma and Bennie van der Brink counted more than 1.5 million Barn Swallows at such a site – one with high grass on a mountain slope in south-east Nigeria. It must have been spectacular to see more than a million swallows dive into the grass within ten minutes around sunset. As they flew up just before daybreak – once again within a ten-minute span – it seemed as if the grass was on fire. Clouds of swallows like rising smoke.

But if House Martins behaved like Swifts, they would not sleep in the reeds, nor in the grass, but high on the wing in the sky. Swifts that sit on eggs, or have chicks to feed, naturally sleep in the shelter of their nests, but birds without nests – and there are quite a few not-yet-breeding juvenile Swifts on the wing in summer – take off until they have reached an altitude of two to three kilometres by nightfall.

In summer, weather radar stations in the Netherlands clearly show that at dusk the Swifts' echoes, which can be recognised by eight wing beats per second, alternated with a brief wing pause, definitely move higher. Around midnight the birds cruise down to altitudes between 500 and 1,000 metres but, before daybreak, once again they climb to at least two kilometres, where they hang around for another hour.

Just like Swifts, House Martins tend to forage at high altitude during the day and seem to be adapted to the cold air: from two kilometres upward the temperature drops below freezing. While Swifts keep their toes tucked away between their belly feathers to prevent them from cooling too much, House Martins' legs are too large for that; they always stick out a bit. It may well be for this reason that House Martins are the only hirundines with feathered legs. Could the feathers act as socks, providing insulation for when temperatures plummet at night?

House Martins hardly ever seem to get caught at typical swallow roosting sites. The Italian bird expert Fernando Spina told me that among the 150,000 Barn Swallows that were caught in southern Europe within the framework of an international migration research project, only a few House Martins were ever captured. Unlike Barn Swallows, House Martins tend to avoid perching in trees, unless occasionally taking shelter in bad weather. If after a stiflingly hot summer day a thunderstorm's rain comes pouring down from heaven, then some House Martins may land on a branch, as on 18 July, 2006 when Petra and I saw around a dozen martins settle in the large ash tree next to our house.

So, in answer to the question of where House Martins go for the night if they don't have a nest, I can only hint at an answer. The truth remains somewhat of a mystery.

Mud cottages and clay thieves

Traditionally – and as we have seen this goes back at least to the Greece of Aristotle around 300 BC – people have greatly admired the creative drive of swallows and martins. Their ability to build a well-shaped round nest from wet lumps of clay: could this be anything but an example for mankind?

House Martins prefer to build their own nests with clay rather than take advantage of man-made versions, a fact we see played out each year on the Old School in Gaast. There, nicely in a row, are 42 beautiful, clean, luxurious House Martin bungalows made of composite timber–concrete, all ready for occupancy, but there is no way the birds want to raise a family there! Only when summer is in full swing and those House Martins which haven't yet started to breed feel the pressure mounting, do we see a few pairs visit the timber–concrete nests. As mentioned previously, we have had no more than six artificial nests occupied in any of the last 12 years.

Nesting always starts with a House Martin that clings to a wall while singing. If an old nest is available, then the vocalist sings out of the entrance hole. Note that the 'singing' of martins and swallows needs qualification. In the late 19th century, the Frisian author Waling Dykstra compared chattering womenfolk to 'swallows on a beanstalk.' And that is exactly what a 'singing' House Martin sounds like. It's rather like jabbering, close to the babbling of a mountain stream, yet in House Martins this jabbering is mostly a male thing.

If a female shows interest, then the first wet lumps of clay are stuck to the wall at the bottom of what could turn into a complete nest cup. The placement of clay lumps and the males babbling while clinging to the wall may carry on for a couple of days. However, if things get serious between a male and a female, it soon shows, as both will begin to build a platform, the base of the nest.

Early in the morning, preferably on fine sunny days, there is much toing and froing of birds gathering mud from the bank of a ditch or from puddles on a farm or a building site. In contrast to their behaviour during the rest of the year, the martins will land on the ground for an instant to quickly scoop up some wet clay with their beak. It has been said that House Martins have to get their wet clay from within 200 metres of the nest location, or the mud will dry out too much in flight. Back on their gradually expanding nest platform, their vibrating little heads mould the fresh clay to the material they have already placed. During the afternoons the fresh layer is allowed to dry.

For the fastest builders it takes up to ten days to complete a brand-new clay cottage from scratch, but the average House Martin pair needs three weeks to build the complete nest from the first lumps of clay to a round shape that has only a tiny opening to allow access. This hole is normally so narrow that the birds need to squeeze themselves flat to get through.

The clay nest consists of around 1,000 clay lumps – give or take a couple of hundred, for the size of a nest does vary. A wet lump of clay weighs something like half a gram, so to build a nest, each House Martin must transport at least half a pound of clay (15 times its own body weight), over an extended period of honest endeavour.

While most martins play by the rules, there are exceptions and I saw my first 'thief' at work on 2 June 2007 while observing the construction of a nest on the east wall. On nest number 33, which was one third complete, a bird was chopping around with its beak, a very different action from the gentle, accurate vibrations with which House Martins fix lumps of clay. Suddenly the House Martin took off with a substantial piece of clay in its beak. Clearly it was an outsider to this colony and as more nests were under construction, the clay thief was able to pull off the trick at two more unfinished nests at least. The thief was actually chased when caught in the act, but less aggressively than if sex had been involved.

Since that first sighting in 2007 I have only come across clay thieves four more times, always in the second half of May or during the first days of June. Perhaps there is no great need for theft in Gaast, as our village is built on clay and all around it there is enough material. In sandy areas it would be a different situation altogether. Indeed, Marten Sikkema related that in a newly developed building estate on the sands, his family had breeding House Martins on the house only for as long as a ditch, newly dug through a loam layer, remained free of vegetation. As soon as plants covered the banks, the House Martins disappeared.

In the Dutch province of Drenthe, where wet clay is notoriously scarce, House Martins made the best of a difficult job by using dirt wetted by horse pee. The nest was kept together by the long black hairs from horses manes and tails (and the support of a plank on which it was built).

Bedclothes

Let's return once more to my morning coffee break on 2 June 2007. A white feather comes spiralling down from the sky near the colony and is neatly taken in flight by an agile House Martin. The martin, feather in beak, immediately gets chased aggressively by another, but at top speed he dives into the entrance hole of a nest of which the clay-work has only just been finished. He? It seems that among House Martins it is mainly the males who bring feathers to the nest.

As soon as the nest structure is completely finished – to my judgement at least – the martins bring along straws, pieces of grass and feathers for a couple of days. Sometimes the straws get carried in so prematurely that they become part of the clay wall. Occasionally House Martins use pieces of string for their nest, just as the birds in Drenthe used the long black hairs of horses' tails or manes.

That this can be rather dangerous is illustrated by a story about a House Martin that perished at Gerrit Twijnstra's house in a nearby Frisian village, It Heidenskip. A piece of pink baler twine was worked into one of the nests. However, bits popped out through the nest's wall. One of the martins was so naïve as to put its head through a loop. This is how Gerrit found the victim of what almost seemed like a suicide.

Similar tragedies occur more often. One morning in Gaast the occupant of a house saw a martin dangling on a 'noose' – a long, thin spear of hay that protruded from the entrance. Probably the bird had trapped itself in its own nesting material while flying out. It was rather morbid to notice that this slowly spinning 'bird scarer' did not upset the other House Martins in any visible way. The inhabitants of the other five nests – which had been built into one bulky construction just under the rafters – flew to and fro regardless. A 'hung martin' was also part of the scene at a large colony in El Rocio, a village in the heart of the Doñana, southern Spain.

Generally the feathers get dragged into the nest during the days of egg laying (the reason why feather collection is the job of the male) to serve as a bed for the brooding House Martins. Research carried out on Tree Swallows in North America (remember that these breed in nest boxes) showed that nests with more feathers had chicks growing faster and becoming larger than chicks in boxes with fewer feathers. Such chicks were also less prone to fleas, mites, and other blood parasites.

This is interesting and may have something to do with the fact that in Tree Swallows, Barn Swallows, House Martins and other swallow-like species the preferred colour for nest feathers tends to be white. Brown and black feathers are rare. The white feathers must be collected from the chickens or the geese in the village, or from the gulls and the terns that breed in the vicinity. White feathers can also be obtained by taking them away from other birds: feather thieves! Many air raids are carried out over white feathers.

Growing up in a horse family, I knew that white hooves are not as strong as black ones. Keratin, the material that makes up a horse's hoof is identical to that which makes up a feather, as well as hair and nails, and this made me wonder for years why House Martins would prefer the white feathers over the black feathers for their nest lining. Surely, black feathers would insulate the nest longer and better?

I now know that the decay of white feathers is controlled by bacteria which thrive on the pale ones (and tend to struggle on black and brown feathers), but on top of this they are capable of something completely different. These bacteria produce chemicals that are particularly harmful to other bacteria that live by accessing the proteins and fats inside birds' eggs. A group of Spanish researchers divided feathers between Barn Swallows' nests, so that part of these nests only contained white feathers, and the others only black ones. This is how they proved that white feathers ensure that eggs are less easily infected by dangerous bacteria. This explains why martins and swallows are so interested in white bedclothes: they have antiseptic qualities!

Rules for nest sanitation appear to change after the eggs have hatched. Early in August 2013, after a fortnight of extremely fine weather, I noticed that the ground beneath the colonies was strewn with white feathers, presumably to reduce temperatures within the nests. In scientific circles it was already known that Barn Swallows eject white feathers during a spell of warm weather and it seems House Martins appear to do the same.

Sex and violence

Like a true paparazzo I've prowled for many hours, but have never seen House Martins mate – as they seem to do it in the privacy of their clay nests. When I was still in nappies, a Swedish-speaking Finn, E.A. Lind, investigated House Martins in Finland. Like me, so many years later, he made his observations from a garden chair and on ten occasions he managed to observe House Martins mate in nests of which the entrance hole was still large enough. The fact that such mating always took place very early in the morning could well be the reason why I have missed out over the past 12 years. I truly regret not being an early bird, as nature is at its best just after daybreak.

Lind says that he witnessed the mating in the days before the laying of the first egg – a period in which females are fertile. On such days unrest sweeps through the colony, not only in the evenings or the mornings, but also during the day. Birds hang halfway out of their entrance hole to keep an eye on everything. It must be the males that have the greatest reason to know whether their neighbour is at home or not. A story from one of the summer supplements of the local newspaper springs to mind. It describes a drunk adolescent rambling across a popular camp site on the island of Terschelling at night, lamenting: "Are there virgins who want to become mothers?" In my perception this is exactly what those House Martins, balancing at their entrance holes, are thinking. Well, perhaps their thoughts are more about the fertility of the females next door rather than about them being virgins.

Adultery may explain why a male I caught one evening in a nest on the old vicarage in Gaast exited a nest at the village hall the next morning, 50 metres down the road. And it may also explain why during such wild days some House Martins may dive into various entrance holes within short intervals and why there is so much fighting going on around the nests.

An unremitting, rasping sound draws attention to birds which are being pushed out of a nest where obviously they didn't belong. Sometimes such an intruder, moaning and rasping, dangles from the nest for another minute before he frees himself. The bouncer clutches a leg or a wing; sometimes he doesn't let go. The fighting duo may stumble out of the nest together and continue their disagreement in mid-air. It even happens that a fighting twosome forgets to fly and falls to the ground. Then one can only hope that the cat's away.

For House Martins it is clear whether they are dealing with a male or a female. I even suspect that all House Martins breeding in Gaast – there are 200 or more of them – know one another by name or nickname. Unfortunately, we lack such power of discernment. Mr Lind was able to distinguish gender by sound in 22 out of 26 nests. The female supposedly has a higher pitch than the male. Even so, Lind claimed that in four couples the call of the two partners sounded identical to him.

Over time I have caught and measured many House Martins. As far as body size is concerned, the sexes are alike, but in the hand the sexes can be distinguished by the colour and feathering of the belly. Females have a bald, red and somewhat wrinkled belly skin: the brood patch. Covered with small downy feathers, the male's breeding spot is not as bald, not as red and not as wrinkled: it has a lower blood flow. The warming of the eggs and the chicks is therefore primarily a female task, but as usual, there are exceptions to this rule. We found a few males with bald, red brood patches, proving emancipation occurs even in House Martins! Because of this we always determine sex by genetic testing based on a drop of blood.

By the way, male adultery leads to what may well be the most obvious sexual marker: the size of the cloaca. This is the body part that ends with the single rear opening of birds. During the breeding season males have twice as wide a cloaca as females – half a centimetre rather than two or three millimetres. This is because males develop structures around the cloacal opening to produce fluids and to store sperm. This indicates the existence of 'sperm competition': the subversive combat between the local martin males for successful impregnations.

Bennie van den Brink sent me a photo of a male raping an unsuspecting female collecting a lump of clay in a puddle. If a male manages to mate with a female, then she receives a big dose of sperm. However private the mating of martins usually may be, extramarital offspring can be found in three out of four nests.

Enough sex talk; let's discuss the result, the offspring.

Cold blood

During the two- to three-week incubation period, it is quiet in the colony. Dads help with the brooding, so there is no fuss, no fights; there is not much to be seen near the nest entrances. As soon as one House Martin returns to the nest, the partner comes out and takes off for his or her turn to hunt for insects in flight. Every 20 to 30 minutes males and females change places. Now and again a bird briefly peeps out through the entrance hole, and occasionally you can see tail-tips moving. If the latter occurs more frequently, you can bet that the eggs are about to hatch.

The typical clutch is four or five eggs, which get laid in the morning, one a day. Normally, incubation starts immediately so that the first egg hatches well before the last one. Even after all eggs have hatched one of the parents remains on the nest, because for the first five days the chicks are bald and need the warmth of a brood patch to maintain body temperature.

The first thing that indicates eggs have hatched is the increase of activity at the entrance. A parent bird will fly in and soon fly out again with a faecal sac for the period when the chicks are too small to successfully eject their waste out of the nest entrance. During this time they deliver their faeces wrapped in white gelatinous tissue so that the parents can remove the bags of chick-poo from the nest.

As soon as the adults are clear of the entrance hole the birds drop the 'filled nappies' from their beak. Such a parcel once landed in my coffee, which wasn't that appetising. After five to six days the chicks are able to turn around in the nest, and with their bums facing the entrance they can deal with domestic hygiene matters for themselves.

I have never rummaged through House Martin nests to see how the young are faring. Firstly, this is rather risky with natural clay nests which can break quite easily, but secondly it wasn't necessary, as various scientists have already made studies of young House Martins lodged in sturdy artificial nests.

Chicks only weigh one gram when they crawl out of the eggshell. They are naked and blind, but tend to come on rapidly during the first few days; after a week they already weigh more than ten grams. If all goes well they start to develop feathers at this point; three weeks old and their weight has reached an amazing 24 grams. 'Amazing,' because this is much heavier than the parents, and indeed much heavier than they will be themselves once they turn into fledglings.

After having reached their maximum weight at three weeks of age, the chicks stay in the nest for another fortnight. They still get fed by the parents, but not as much as before. Gradually their weight decreases, but their feathers continue to grow. After five weeks, if the weather has been kind and at the time that fledglings start leading their own life on the wing, they weigh only around 17 grams. In a cold, wet, gusty spell, the parents usually have a hard time to provide enough insects, so the development of the young can come to a halt and the entire process is delayed.

At first it may seem rather contradictory, but if you believe the scientists that studied the phenomenon, House Martins are actually well adapted to bad weather in summer. During cool, rainy and windy days when there is little to eat, chicks immediately adjust their body temperature to the outside air, dropping into a drowsy state and barely managing to raise their little heads when mum or dad manages to bring some food to the nest. By turning off the 'central heating' they save a lot of energy. If energy is that scarce, the young prioritise the development of 'structural body parts' such as the skeleton and wings. The deficiency in body weight can be taken care of later.

After ten days or so, House Martin chicks are capable of regulating their own body temperature. Because the development of the down has increased during the second week, they now have their own insulation. With their broad yellow beaks they then sit chirpily in front of the entrance for the first time, waiting for a parent with food. During this time they look like those critical old men from the Muppet Show: Statler and Waldorf. They have a bald skull, with bits of down sticking out from both sides.

Apropos of this hairdo, most birds keep the down around their heads for quite a while. Young Red Knots and Black-tailed Godwits, for instance, may already be able to fly, and still wear such tufts of fluff. In the eyes of humans this makes them cute and chick-like. Perhaps their parents agree, as they are persuaded to carry on protecting and pampering their offspring for a while.

Martins in infancy

Even though they get fed less and less, young House Martins will remain in the nest for a couple of weeks after they lose that cute fluffy hair. Often there are four or even five in a brood, but only two – sometimes three – can fit into the entrance hole to await the delivery of a fly-meal. Generally they change places peacefully, but sometimes a fight breaks out with a young House Martin pecking vigorously at its sibling. Not a pleasant sight.

Perhaps such fights occur mainly after cold days when it has been difficult for the parents to gather enough flies. During such days, the youngsters may have had to live off their fat stores, with lowered body temperature, and maybe when things are really tough even their parents have to turn down the thermostat.

Normally House Martins have a core body temperature of 40 degrees Celsius, so a drop down to 25 degrees Celsius would be a great test for a youngster, increasing its vulnerability outside the safety of the nest. This was apparent on the afternoon of 18 August 2012 when my neighbours Karin and Cathy came to the house with a juvenile House Martin in a shoebox. Cathy had found the youngster on her doorstep, presumably a refugee from the large colony next door. Pitying the little bird, they have come to see the 'specialist.' The tiny creature cries out as we pick it up. It refuses to fly, but it is lively enough so we decide to put it into an empty nest in view of Cathy's front door. At the top of the ladder I carefully hold the little martin level with the entrance hole. At first it resists, but then it suddenly slips into the empty nest and stays put. Hopefully it manages to call out to its parents and get fed long enough to take off into the skies on its own.

Once a backpacker found such a House Martin chick below a nest at the home of Ruurdtsje and Thom de Boer. The girl had immediately phoned the Dutch RSPCA for assistance, but well before the rescue team arrived from a nearby city, Ruurdtsje and Thom had put the young House Martin back in one of the nests. "Cancel the ambulance", Thom had told her, but this message came too late. Just like the rescue team itself.

Some juveniles, usually the ones that hatched last, lose the battle for life. They tend to be smaller and not quite strong enough to secure a place at the entrance hole so miss out on getting fed when supplies are short. Sometimes you find such a juvenile beneath the colony; perhaps pushed out of the nest by its siblings or even a parent. To us these things are hard to accept, but in terms of hard evolutionary logic they are understandable. The fourth and the fifth egg can be regarded as 'reproductive insurance.' At the time of egg-laying the martins cannot predict the subsequent weather, and individuals that lay five eggs raise more offspring in fine summers.

The older they get, the more the young martins hang out of the nest during the day. The agile little heads with the feisty dark eyes keep a close eye on their surroundings. It is inevitable: soon they will fledge but those first flights need to be done properly, as a non-flying House Martin away from the protection of the nest soon becomes a dead House Martin.

During the last couple of weeks up in the nest, the juveniles train their muscles, for instance by vibrating their wings. Physically they are getting ready for take-off. Their built-in flight systems take care of a lot, but that does not mean that they shouldn't try to follow one of their parents very carefully on their maiden flight.

During a fine summer, many House Martins feel the urge to start a second brood, but for that to happen the first batch must have left the nest. Ruurdtsje de Boer told me that she saw how parents tried to lure their young out of the nest. They tempt their offspring by hovering mid-air in front of the entrance (excuse me, exit) hole, and continuously grazing their youngsters' heads that protrude from the nest opening. They encourage them by calling out something like: 'Come along!' Of course this is an interpretation. But it made me feel good to find various references in the hirundine literature to the ways in which martins and swallows tempt the juveniles to fly. Ruurdtsje was right.

After their maiden flight juveniles will return to their nest. They are still being fed, as even fully fledged House Martins are experts at begging. Their cheekiness increases constantly and they start visiting other parts of the colony where they may get fed in (empty) nests in which they were not born. They inspect ruined old nests, sit on a freshly constructed base for a new nest, and peep into holes in the wall. They have plenty of time to practise the art of 'clinging' to a wall and eventually they get chased off by the neighbours.

Early in summer the juveniles stay close to the colony for a couple of weeks and in the evenings they return to the nest to sleep with mum, dad and the second brood. One evening after nightfall I placed balls of soft paper in a few entrance holes. The next morning I cleared the openings and caught the birds that escaped into a plastic bag. I was amazed to capture as many as seven or eight birds, not counting the small chicks that remained inside the nest. In Finland, E.A. Lind once counted up to 11 sleeping House Martins – nine juveniles and two parents – in a single nest.

Occasionally I have tried to imagine the goings-on in a nest at night. Martins bundled up in a tight space, who would surely like to turn over once in a while during their sleep. Judging by the murmuring sound of their conversations they do more than just sleep during the night. One of the consequences of this behaviour became clear as Jeanet and Maaike, sisters of Jacob de Groot whom we have met in the first chapter, appeared at the door with a pair of skinny but very alive House Martins.

They had found the pair underneath a row of nests at their house, unable to move because they were attached to one another. The mother's outer quill was tightly entangled with the daughter's outer quill. They were skinny, and might have been trying to free themselves all day before they tumbled out of the nest and were found. Clearly, the cat had been away. We carefully untangled the quills, ringed the martins, and took a small blood sample – that is why I am so sure that they were mother and daughter. When released, both birds flew off fine.

As I looked at their entangled tails I was reminded of a story by the famous Dutch author and trained biologist Maarten 't Hart, a story that obviously made a rather big impression. I read it in his book *Ratten* (*Rats*) at secondary school. It was about the 'king of the rats' – the phenomenon of five or ten or sometimes as many as 25 black rats, found alive or dead with their tails in a knot. (Brown rats have shorter tails which don't get tangled.) With their tails in knots the rats are trapped until they starve to death. 't Hart explains that such a tangle of tails is the unhappy outcome of a night during which rats share their bodily warmth by bunching up snugly. There is some twisting and wriggling going on and the tails get messed up, especially if they are a bit wet and sticky. This is how it must have happened with these two House Martins too, but this time it had a happy ending.

By the way, going to sleep at night can lead to rather stressful situations. Sometimes the parent House Martins will bar the youngsters from their home. The juveniles themselves also enjoy causing problems for others. For as long as the entrance is blocked, the approach route is taken over and over again. This causes chaos at the entrance hole, with quite a lot of shrieking and shouting in House Martin slang. However, juveniles may also work for a living. Fully fledged young ones that I recognised by the colour of rings around their leg regularly fed their younger siblings in the parental nest. There has even been a sighting of a young House Martin feeding a parent.

Hobbies – an aerial threat

On 27 June 2013 we were alerted by the House Martins' intensive alarm calls to a Marsh Harrier circling low over our village. Shrill tseeps all around us kept going for over a quarter of an hour and that surprised us, for why should House Martins fear such a large, slow bird of prey? Are they perhaps scared of an attack on their nest? Do they want to warn the juveniles, and teach them that such birds can be dangerous?

In the course of summer the chance of such threats increases gradually. Sometimes in June, but more often in July and August, we can expect the small summer falcons, the Hobbies. The House Martins themselves almost always bring them to our attention. If they rush into the air as one flock while tseeping massively, then you can bet your life that a Hobby is going to cross the heavens soon. Or that it is carrying out an air raid there and then. The group disperses, the House Martins come down, and the tseeping stops: all clear!

In early September 2002, it was a warm late-summer day when we moved from Texel to Gaast. That afternoon, after we'd unpacked the van and the work was done, we agreed it was time to dive into Lake IJsselmeer, though diving here is not easy: beyond the dyke and past the reed beds, the shallows stretch for at least a mile, so one must wade for quite a while before the water even reaches one's knees. But we managed to get wet and cool down. As we walked down the dyke back to our new home, we heard House Martins alarm high above the village. A short, high-pitched shriek followed. A Hobby had dropped from the sky and captured a martin mid-flight. Most likely a juvenile at its playful age.

With a silhouette like a Swift or a Peregrine Falcon, and a body size between the two, Hobbies are excellent aerobatic aviators and their appetite is considerable. This makes them an obvious and substantial threat to House Martins, even though it takes a considerable effort to catch them. The Hobbies which target our House Martins presumably breed in old nests of Carrion Crows or Magpies in one of the duck decoys a kilometre or so to the north of the village.

Sometimes a Hobby will approach a village by flying slightly above the ground and then, steering clear of houses and trees, launches a surprise attack, but the usual method is to suddenly literally drop from the sky. From almost 1,000 metres a Hobby will fold its wings to plummet at a dazzling speed onto a House Martin. To burst onto the target at 100 kilometres per hour, and still have a failure rate of more than 50%, says much for the speed and agility of House Martins. The House Martins that are caught are almost certainly solitary juveniles who have not yet become experienced flyers.

Despite the difficulties in catching small birds in mid-air, in July and August Hobbies survive largely on them. Top of the menu are Barn Swallows, followed by Swifts and House Martins. Thus, the 'high flyers' contribute the least. That's probably why House Martins, as soon as they spot a Hobby, instantly climb high in the air and keep close to one another at great altitude. They must try and stay above the Hobby.

My friend and source of inspiration Rob Bijlsma not only conducts fine research on birds of prey, Wood Warblers and so much else in the woods of Drenthe, he occasionally carries out field work abroad. In January and February 2001 he was in south-east Nigeria for four weeks. In the mountains near Boje-Ebok among the tropical forests there are slopes covered with elephant grass. This sturdy grass is four to five metres high and every night between one and three million Barn

Swallows sleep in this high grass. As the sun sets, they dive into the grass on the mountain slopes within less than ten minutes. It looks like a tropical downpour of Barn Swallows.

Early in the morning the swallows wake up 20 minutes before dawn. A prattling sound builds up until they burst out of the grass a few minutes before sunrise. According to Rob they immediately fly at top speed. Some fly downhill and accelerate while skimming the elephant grass. They avoid the open space above the grass, for that is much too dangerous. Most of them take off vertically, spiralling and at full speed. After this they become invisible for the rest of the day.

Such aerobatics are definitely not meant to impress; the Barn Swallows fly in this way to keep out of the talons of Hobbies and other birds of prey. Every morning and every evening these raptors head for where millions of prey birds are gathering! Yet, a Hobby hardly manages to catch more than one or two swallows a day. During the course of one winter a dozen Hobbies can only devour a few thousand swallows. So the average Barn Swallow in Boje-Ebok has a 0.1% chance of being eaten by a Hobby in winter.

House Martins do not 'drop' into elephant grass in the evening. Maybe they spend the night high up in the sky. Or maybe they hide somewhere else. In some dredge spoils near Gaast? Or somewhere in Africa, after all?

Louse flies

All right, as a graduate in biology I am not supposed to ascribe any human characteristics to animals, but I make an exception for the louse fly. Scared, cowardly, chicken-hearted lice – that's what they are! What am I talking about? About wingless flies with spindly little legs that live off the blood of House Martins.

You can describe them as tiny martin-Draculas, though they are not that small. If you look at them from above, their diameter is at least five millimetres. Next to a little Barn Swallow which measures ten centimetres in length and three in width, they are obviously big guys. And they live off the half gram of blood that runs through a House Martin.

My interest in louse flies got a boost when during a wader meeting I discovered that my Scottish friend and fellow wader enthusiast, Ron Summers, had been studying louse flies for an undergraduate project in the early 1970s. And the great thing was that he published an account of it too, the paper in *Journal of Zoology* still representing one of the rare investigations of louse fly ecology!

Louse flies are rather plump, inelegant insects, unless you fall for the six slender and agile legs. They are flat and hairy and have a short piercing mouthpart to get to the blood. Louse flies have no wings – just vestigial stumps that help them keep their balance. When sucking blood, the rear part of their body swells like that of a tick.

The most remarkable feature of louse flies is that they keep their offspring – that is to say, their eggs and larvae – inside their bodies. The fertilised eggs are not laid to the outside; they land in a type of louse fly uterus where they hatch. Inside the uterus the larvae are fed with louse fly milk from special glands. Louse fly mothers thus process the fresh House Martin blood before they deliver it to their offspring.

Only after the larvae pupate in the rear part of her body will the mother 'lay' them – pupae that look like small, shiny, dark brown 'eggs'. About two millimetres in diameter, the brown chrysalis hibernates at the bottom of the clay nests, primarily in the cracks between the nest and the wall or the woodwork. As the House Martins return in spring, the young louse flies are waiting for them in the old nests to start a new cycle.

Louse flies on House Martins are so specific that they will not bite humans, nor Swifts, which have their own specific Swift louse fly. Barn Swallows have yet another louse fly, at least I think so. I don't know if it hurts when you get bitten by a louse fly, but what I do know is that their way of crawling is very itchy. The louse flies are active in the nest, but like little travellers on bird backs, they accompany the House Martins on their flights around the colony.

If you catch House Martins you will not find many louse flies. Only one in 20 carries a single one, and only very rarely will you find as many as eight or ten. If you hold such a martin in your hand, the lice seem to panic. At least, they run around among the feathers, perhaps to get out of sight or they escape by running along a human forearm. The latter is rather foolish, because if they had stayed among the feathers we wouldn't have noticed them at all. Now we do. And so we lend the House Martins a hand by gathering louse flies. They are put in alcohol in the name of science.

Disloyal chicken-hearted lice I called them. This refers to the way they abandon the sinking ship – the House Martin that has been captured and is handled. Occasionally – it has happened to me twice – a louse fly will fall out of the sky without announcement, presumably dislodged from a flying House Martin. Whether it landed in my hair or between my clothes, I immediately got an itching feeling because our relatively hairless skin has many sensors. Birds have tactile senses at the base of their feathers, so perhaps House Martins do not sense any irritation. Perhaps they don't even feel the snout bite, which would explain why at our place the House Martins always prefer to reoccupy dirty old clay nests that have survived winter rather than clean artificial nests.

In spring, in each of these nests in Gaast around 20 louse flies will be waiting for the birds' return. I know this because I have done a count. One winter I knocked all the nests off one wall and counted the chrysalises. A House Martin's motto is: 'rather an old home with louse flies than a luxurious man-made bungalow'. The fact that biologists have looked in vain for negative effects of louse flies on mature and juvenile House Martins and Swifts tallies well with this story.

Malaria

Louse flies are not the only insects that make a living on House Martin blood. Clay nests can be chock-a-block with fleas, and because of the incidence of malaria parasites in House Martin populations, it is almost certain that House Martins are bitten by mosquitoes. Young birds born in Europe might still be free of the type of blood parasites which in humans cause malaria but, once they return in spring, one third of the House Martins in Gaast carries malaria parasites. During a martin's lifespan the risk of infection only increases.

Malaria is a tropical disease caused by unicellular parasites that eat blood cells – and sometimes even the liver cells of humans. Such parasites rupture organic tissue for their own benefit. By getting as many as possible of them – in their next stage of development – into their host's blood stream, the malarial parasites increase the chance that they will be sucked up again by a female mosquito looking for a blood meal. The mosquito uses this blood to produce eggs which it deposits in still, open water. If a mosquito sucks blood from two martins, there is a good chance that malaria parasites are passed on from one victim to the next.

Just like louse flies, malaria parasites specialise in specific types of 'hosts.' Malarial blood parasites of humans do not occur in most other animals, and those in the House Martin tend to belong to

House Martins alone. But certain types of malaria they share with other birds. How do we know all this?

Malarial parasites are invisible to the naked eye but infected red blood cells can be examined under an ordinary optical microscope. This type of research is quite a job, for infected cells tend to be rare and it is fairly easy to miss a malaria infection. The success rate increases when you look for the parasite's genetic material: the malaria DNA.

This also starts with a drop of blood preserved in alcohol – one could also use Dutch genever or English gin. The DNA that can be drawn from a blood sample is mainly House Martin DNA; only a very small amount of parasite DNA may show. Once you know the unique codes of certain bits of parasite DNA – codes that do not occur in House Martins – then you can multiply these. This is how even the smallest malaria infection can be brought to light.

I was lucky enough to be able to work alongside Marco van der Velde, a fellow Frisian biologist, and a close colleague at the University of Groningen. I took blood samples and Marco dealt with the DNA. This is how we learned that the House Martins carried at least seven different types of malarial parasites; that half of the House Martins carried more than one type; and that the oldest martins carried the greatest variety of malaria parasites. When returning to Gaast after a year, it is likely that a House Martin has added another little parasite to its collection.

Perhaps you've noticed that I keep referring to malaria parasites and not to 'malaria'. This is because 'malaria' stands for the disease, not the parasites. Marco and I have seriously tried to find indications of our martins suffering from malaria by checking to see if they are smaller or lighter, or less likely to return the next year. The data have spoken loud and clear: the House Martins of Gaast do not suffer from carrying malarial parasites.

The same applied to House Martins in the south of Spain, but… only if a single variety of malaria was involved. Unlike the situation in Friesland, Spanish House Martins did suffer when they were infected by two types of malaria.

How can we explain the difference between the Spanish and the Frisian martins? And another puzzle: where do these House Martins get infected by malaria in the first place? The fact that we have never found an infection on juveniles means that the mosquitoes in our village do not spread any martin malaria. Some of the malaria varieties that Marco found in our House Martins indicate that they are spread by mosquitoes in Africa, so we need to understand what happens there in winter.

Insect-eating orcas

Try to image you are a fly, a fat blowfly sitting on the roof-gutter of the church when you smell cows. Cows, that means cow dung, food. Let's go for it! Halfway through your trip to the cows a big black-and-white beast with an enormous beak emerges out of the blue. It's too late already: you've disappeared inside that beak.

Now multiply the weight of this blowfly and the black-and-white beast 200,000 times, so that the fly now weighs the same as a human being. Of course, a fly as heavy as that can't fly, but it can swim and might potentially come across an orca, a killer whale… What I want to point out is that a fly compares to a swallow-like bird as a human to an orca and when you are as small as a fly, then the air is almost as viscous as water. Luckily House Martins eat a lot more flies than killer whales eat humans.

I started the orca analogy because when I look at a House Martin, it often reminds me of them: black on top, white underneath. A flat face with a broad beak and dark beady eyes hidden away in the black just before it touches the white. When they peep at me, with their little heads sticking out of the nest, the House Martins are just tiny killer whales.

Perhaps surprisingly it is not mere coincidence that House Martins and orcas look so alike. In both animals the contrast between the black on top and the white underneath 'serves a purpose', meaning there is a sound biological reason for it. Thanks to the black-and-white pattern both orcas and House Martins live 'in their own shadow', so that a fly in the air and a human – or a seal – in the water can hardly see the large predator approaching.

Technically referred to as 'countershading', the white belly of a killer whale or a House Martin doesn't stand out against the light of the sky, just as its black back blends in with its dark surroundings when looked at from above. There is hardly any contrast and therefore the entire object is rather difficult to spot. Snap! – eaten by such a black-and-white beast before you could see it coming.

House Martins eat all sorts of flying insects and drifting spiders, but not bees, wasps, butterflies, dragonflies, damselflies and hardly any beetles. They certainly eat flies in an abundance of varieties. The list of possible prey types is rather long and daunting for a non-entomologist like me. In 1962 a German biologist, Kurt von Gunten, made the first serious analysis of a House Martin's diet and treated his readers to six full pages of insect photographs.

Here, a simpler story will do just fine. Studies from the Czech Republic, Germany, England and Scotland have shown that a large majority of these flying creatures consists of flies, mosquitoes, and aphids. Black Bibionidae flies which live in grassy areas make up a substantial portion of the menu. Bibionid flies play an important role in the pollination of meadow flowers and their larvae feed on rotting material between the roots.

How do we know so much about the diet of House Martins when it is not possible for us on the ground to observe what they are catching? The answers are provided when the adult birds fly into the nest to feed young ones with a throat packed with fly-mash. Like meatballs, these fly-pellets disappear into the wide-open, broad yellow beaks of the begging chicks. By tying a piece of string around a chick's neck a researcher can retrieve the food parcel. (You'll be pleased to learn that in their publications the researchers state that the chicks were rewarded with bits of minced meat after their pellets had been taken away from them.)

If you were prepared to examine their poo, you would not need to harass the chicks. It is easy to get underneath the nests; from each insect at least something indigestible remains inside the faeces. After some study, each and every insect can be recognised by a bit of leg, a bit of exoskeleton, or half a wing.

Swallow-like species all eat mosquitoes and aphids, but with distinct preferences between them. Barn Swallows, for instance, eat few aphids. There is a good reason for this, because Barn Swallows fly close to the ground, and aphids 'on the move' climb up in the air. In fact, the higher up you go, the smaller the insects. Hence, Swifts and House Martins have to make do with a lot of tiny bites; Barn Swallows eat fewer but larger prey.

Barn Swallows tend to perch between foraging flights. From a branch of an alder bush they may hunt for insects passing by. Like a flycatcher they make a short pursuit, and go back to the branch. Swifts and House Martins never do this. Should they be waiting for insects passing by, they would soar against the wind with still wings.

Here comes the crux: Barn Swallows are not *able* to soar. They are more heavily built than House Martins. With their shorter wings and their longer, deeply forked tails they are designed for high speed and great manoeuvrability. Barn Swallows fly almost 50% faster than House Martins and their take-off is faster too. Barn Swallows have a minimal turning circle of 1.5 metres, whereas House Martins need at least two metres.

It still amazes me that as early as 1773, in a world without binoculars and fast-shutter-speed cameras, Gilbert White could sketch the contrast between House Martins and Barn Swallows so accurately. Let me give him the word: "*Martins are by far the least agile of the four [swallow-like] species; their wings and tails are short, and therefore they are not capable of such surprising turns and quick and glancing evolutions as the swallow. Accordingly they make use of the placid easy motion in a middle region of the air, seldom mounting to any great height, and never sweeping long together over the surface of the ground or the water.*"

In summer you can watch the House Martins performing turns all the time. Some House Martins seem to turn only clockwise and others only anti-clockwise. Some of the House Martins that I handle during the annual bird-ringing season have tails that curve sideways. Quills seem to be bent either one way or another, even in some of the recently fledged juveniles, and one day I hope I'll be able to prove if the tails adjust to an individual's tendency to turn right or left. By marking the bellies of the birds with dots of paint, you could actually compare the direction of tail curvature with the way they turn in the sky.

Obviously insects will do anything to avoid being caught and devoured by swallows and martins. They have two tactics: either a high-speed escape or a drop to the ground. During flight, birds depend on the up-current beneath their wings, so it is easier for them to turn up rather than down. That is why House Martins often catch insects by turning upward.

Like killer whales in the sea, they approach their prey from below. When this happens high in the sky, an insect can try to let itself drop, but usually without success. Close to the ground this tactic usually means the insect lands safely in the grass, which is why Barn Swallows, who hunt for food much nearer to the ground than House Martins, need such speed and aerobatics. It is one or the other.

At home in Gaast the Barn Swallows fly around the village in summer, and the House Martins fly above it. Barn Swallows only move a couple of hundred metres away from their nest and House Martins also try to keep close to their nests, because this saves time and flying effort when feeding their nestlings.

On warm days – this has been known for centuries – swallows and martins will fly higher than usual, which is why they are regarded as weather predictors. 'Low flies the swallow, rain to follow. When swallows fly high the weather will be dry.'

Personally, I question if hirundines do predict changes in the weather by changing altitude. I rather believe that they only react to such changes. This is rather an easy one to check. Keep daily records of the weather and the altitudes of flight in House Martins and swallows, and see whether flight height correlates with the weather of the day, or the weather of tomorrow.

Shakespeare and the sweet scent of dung

Eelke Scherjon represented the fifth generation of clog-making Scherjons and his wife Marie and sons Hannes and Jilles are now in charge of the thriving little company in Noardburgum, their distinctive brown-dabbed, black-based clogs, widely famous as 'Scherjontsjes', being a pleasure to wear (I do this at home).

Not only did Hannes and Jilles, the sixth generation, inherit his craft (and in Hannes' case, his dyke-vaulting sport), they also treasure the swallows. In Eelke's time, in 2007, the first Barn Swallows started nesting in the white-painted hall where four clog-makers operate especially designed (but noisy) machines to turn blocks of willow wood into clog shapes. Ever since, as soon as the first swallows are spotted in April, one window is removed to allow the birds free access to the building and from May to early September the clog-makers share their head-space with Barn Swallows. With more than ten pairs and their young in 2014, it has become rather busy. Outdoors, the Swallows on the wing, catching insects over small fields surrounded by trees, lead the way to the clog-makery. It makes for a very lively kind of industry.

These are the facts about the aeroplanktonic food of the hirundines: the higher the temperature, the more insects are airborne. Close to the ground there are more insects near wood fringes than in open countryside. And in bad weather the numbers of insects near wood fringes drop less rapidly than over open fields. That's why House

Martins struggle sooner from bad weather than Barn Swallows; House Martins simply don't manage to fly fast enough to catch insects at ground level. On cold days and with strong winds, the House Martins of Gaast flee to the vast borders of Lake IJsselmeer, where small insects continue to appear over the reedbeds. Only in cases of emergency do birds leave the village.

Occasionally they may travel even farther from home. House Martins may deliberately approach an imminent thunderstorm, because just ahead of such a squall the rising air mass causes a concentration of flying insects. House Martins, along with Swifts, conveniently exploit thunderstorms to fill their stomachs.

Once all this fly-food is devoured, it is transformed into House Martin labour, House Martin growth, and House Martin droppings. Most people dislike House Martin dung. At our house we have about 14 nests just above the bathroom window, so there are summer weeks when about 60 chicks drop their dung on the window sill. Can one smell it? Of course, one can smell it, but does it bother us? No, and less and less so. As soon as it has dried up, the fly-ooze excreted by House Martins has a somewhat sweet scent.

In fact, I would rather not be without this scent. In England, a world-famous author may have come to the same conclusion. Four hundred years ago the sweet scent of martin poo was evocatively described by one on less than William Shakespeare. This is what he says in Macbeth – Act 1, Scene 6:

> *This guest of summer,*
> *The temple-haunting martlet, does approve,*
> *By his loved mansionry that the heaven's breath*
> *Smells wooingly here. No jutty, frieze,*
> *Buttress, nor coign of vantage, but this bird*
> *Hath made his pendant bed and procreant cradle;*
> *Where they most breed and haunt, I have observed,*
> *The air is delicate.*

Singer, songwriter and poet Nynke Laverman translated this verse into Frisian:

> *Dizze simmergast,*
> *De swel, dy't húsmannet yn timpels, ferklearret*
> *Mei't er hjir syn nêst boud hat, de swietrook fan 'e wyn:*
> *Gjin râne, gjin skoar, gjin richel of krûp-yntsje,*
> *Dit bistke hinget der syn broeibêd op:*
> *Dêr't sy it leafst briede en binne, merk ik faak,*
> *Is suvere loft.*

Clearly, in the 1,500 years since starting their separate ways, English and Frisian have drifted apart.

And, surely, orca poo is unlikely to smell this good.

House Martin statistics

When, in 2002, we moved into the Old School in Gaast, there was one old House Martin nest left on the north wall. Indeed, just above that bathroom window. A second nest was added that summer. Clay nests at this side of the house tend to keep well through the winters, and as House Martins prefer to reuse old nests over newly built clay or artificial nests, the numbers kept growing on our north wall.

During the summers 2010 to 2014 we had 14 House Martin couples – and their offspring – defaecating on the bathroom window and the climbing hydrangea. As Petra and I enjoyed its sweet fragrance, the hydrangea enjoyed the extra fertiliser.

The Netherlands National Office of Statistics (CBS) in The Hague is supposed to 'publish reliable and consistent statistical information, which responds to the needs of society.' A prerequisite is added: 'The quality of the statistical information provided must be guaranteed.' The same professional attitude can be found in volunteers who draw up the Gaast House Martin statistics. For more than 25 years, Eelco Brandenburg, in a self-appointed volunteer capacity, has been responsible for the counts of House Martin nests in Gaast and the surrounding villages.

Together with Jan van Dijk, an old mate from Texel, each year I try to catch, recapture and newly ring 50 to 100 House Martins. At our Old School I tally the number of broods raised per pair. The first activity shows the size of the actual House Martin breeding population; the second is essential for the calculation of annual survival rates; the third gives some information on the breeding success of the House Martins of Gaast.

Eelco does his rounds in late July, a time of the year that Jan and I also carry out what we call our 24-hour martin-catching marathon. We start at noon and browse through the village in search of inhabited nests; with hand nets and other netting we try to catch as many as possible of their inhabitants. During the first day we carry on late into the evening; early the next morning we pick up the thread and continue until noon.

Typically, on days like that we tend to catch about 60 House Martins, with the evenings and early mornings producing the highest numbers because the martins are at home. If you move a net in front of the entrance hole, success will be yours, but if you try too late in the evening or too early in the morning the House Martins will stay put in the safety of their nests.

The first time I tried catching House Martins at the Old School I had some help from a friend, the potato farmer and amateur biologist Joop Jukema. It all seemed so straightforward: the House Martins flew into the nets without hesitation and not a single tseep was heard. But it was the last time that things went so smoothly; that very first time the birds had no idea what was coming to them. From then on there have always been birds around to sound the alarm when they recognise either the nets or the catchers – even after a year. It has almost turned into a competition between the House Martins and us. We keep changing the arrangements and the type of nets in an effort to fool the birds.

An experiment carried out with House Martins in Poland demonstrated that the birds keep a good eye on people and form judgements about their motives. They appeared to make a distinction between people who actually look at their nests and people who look away. 'Tseep' sounds only occurred when people looked at nests and in such cases the Polish House Martins refused to return to their nests.

On 30 July 2013 Jan and I experienced such a situation at the house of Lammert and Karin at the end of our street, House Martins nest below a gutter barely more than two metres from the ground. The martins are within easy reach of a hand net and know it, so even when we half-hid ourselves behind the privet hedge, the birds fathomed us and stayed away from their nests as long as possible.

On other occasions the martins can become over confident about recognising potential danger. That same afternoon we went to catch the martins at our house, where the nests are secured five to eight metres above the ground on the eastern wall. Here our technique was to wave a mist-net between two very long sticks and because the House Martins seemed unable to imagine that the two people at ground level could mean 'catching danger' they were easy to capture.

When a House Martin is caught, it is placed in the waiting room – that is to say, a cotton bag. It then receives a small aluminium ring around one of its legs with the inscription Arnhem-VT Holland and a unique code of two letters and five digits, for example AP 10990. Arnhem-VT stands for the Arnhem Vogeltrekstation, *i.e.* the Arnhem bird ringing station. This name is still in use although the Dutch ringing administration moved from Arnhem to Heteren years ago, and is now located in Wageningen. Perhaps surprisingly, if you address a letter to Arnhem-VT in the Netherlands it will still get to the right place. The European bird ringing offices are so well connected that when you try to send the details of a ringed bird to the British Trust for Ornithology (BTO) in Thetford, you will be directed to a 'Euring' interactive website. Try it!

Once a bird has been made into a unique individual by a numbered ring, we weigh it, measure the length of the wing and sternum, and take the length of the inner and outer tail feathers. We also take a drop of blood to provide the DNA that confirms the sex of the bird and informs us about its malarial parasites. Often we also collect the tips from the two innermost primary feathers. As we will see in a minute, the analysis of this tiny amount of feather material can help us find out where House Martins spend the winter.

Of course some of the House Martins we capture will already carry a ring around their leg and by comparing the year-on-year records, it suggests that the Gaast population must be regarded as a single large colony, with House Martins that breed at one end of the village one year being found at the other end 12 months later.

A lot of exchanges take place between the nesting groups at the various houses; all change address each year, but that is not all… almost all change partners each year too, with older birds normally mating with other experienced birds. The younger ones are forced to find other inexperienced partners because the older birds come back to the breeding colony first. By the time the young ones arrive in Gaast, the older birds have settled for an old nest… and an 'elderly' mate!

A recapture proves that a particular House Martin has survived since the previous catch but if a ringed House Martin fails to be recaptured the year after, it doesn't mean that it has died. It may have moved elsewhere permanently or simply managed to avoid our nets in Gaast. As shown by research in Germany, adult House Martins tend to remain faithful to their village. Our calculations show a rather constant adult annual survival rate of 45%, close to estimates obtained previously in Germany and the UK. This gives a breeding House Martin a life expectancy of almost two years. Naturally, the life expectancy of a fledgling is somewhat longer, but not by much. Just around 20% of the young born in Gaast are estimated to survive their first year, but it is quite possible that half of the surviving youngsters have moved off to breed in other villages. If we accept this, the average fledgling House Martins would look forward towards a life lasting about three years.

During our first years in Gaast, from 2002 until 2010, Eelco Brandenburg counted between 150 and 200 nests each summer, though the nests were distributed quite differently across the village from year to year. Initially, the characteristic village corner house, close to the dyke that separates the village from the reed beds bordering Lake IJsselmeer, had the most nests. At times there were more than 40.

After the owner died the house was sold and in late 2005 it was demolished, to be rebuilt the next year. This modern version of the lovely original building attracted a growing number of House Martin nests, with 16 pairs using it in 2012. Sadly, despite being forbidden by Dutch law, the new owners had their nests removed in 2013 and I am quite sure that several displaced House Martins moved over to the Old School.

Since 2010 the number of nests in Gaast has tumbled, with just 101 being recorded in 2013. The decline has occurred all over the Netherlands and seems to be associated with a series of cold summers. Especially in landscapes where insects have become sparse, House Martins will find it hard to cope with low temperatures and stormy, wet weather, as this increases the costs (heat loss of adults and chicks) and reduces the income (the catch of insect aeroplankton). From 2009 to 2012 the months of June were colder and wetter than average. In 2011 and 2012 this was also followed by cold, wet weather in July. In such summers only a quarter of the nests accommodated second broods. This is rather low compared to Gilbert White's suggestion that in Selborne of the 1770s most, if not all, House Martins had second broods. Published evidence from England, Scotland and across mainland Europe from the late 20th century indicated that 60–90% second broods were the rule.

Although the spring of 2013 was icy cold and the House Martins started breeding late, the summer was beautiful and the number of second broods was as high as 60%. As a result I predicted in 2013 that Eelco would walk around Gaast happier again in 2014. With a small increase to 112 pairs, in fact he did!

Squawking blankets over green

When people who hardly know me want to make friendly conversation, they often ask me: 'How are the birds doing?' I find this slightly awkward, for my counter question would be: 'Which birds would you like to talk about?' And what would it mean if I answered 'all right,' or 'poorly'? Is more always better?

With respect to the Barnacle Geese in the meadows around Gaast in winter, most people would say that there are quite enough of them now. Compared to a few decades ago they have indeed become rather numerous. There were only 30,000 Barnacle Geese wintering in the Netherlands when I was a boy, but now there are 20 times as many.

When the geese were rare winter guests they always left in early April for the north; now we see tens of thousands hang around Gaast until the end of May, munching grass that the farmers think is theirs. This is because the grasslands around the Baltic which they would traditionally use as stop-off feeding areas are already full of other geese. Right now most of Friesland's wintering Barnacle Geese must fly non-stop to their north-Russian breeding grounds, but as many encounter difficulties in doing so, rates of reproduction will gradually drop; eventually their population increase will grind to a halt.

No one can fault the way that the Dutch have taken care of our geese, particularly in relation to their food. Our well-fertilised grasslands remain green even in winter, which means that grass is growing, yielding the protein-rich food on which vegetarians such as geese depend. More green grass means more geese. As long as we produce such large amounts of food for them we should not be surprised at their large numbers. As the Frisian comedian Rients Gratama once said: *"Don't moan about taxes – earn less instead"*. As long as we fertilise our pastures so much that the grass keeps growing, we'd better enjoy the huge flocks of geese that fly over Gaast like squawking blankets as they move to or from the shallow shores of Lake IJsselmeer where they drink and sleep.

Whilst the numbers of Barnacle Geese have strongly increased since my youth, the numbers of House Martins have strongly declined. Around 1970 there were an estimated 450,000 breeding House Martin pairs in the Netherlands, but by 1990 only 120,000 pairs remained. A drop of two-thirds of the population has also been measured in England where the decline was most marked in the second half of the 1980s. Unfortunately the tide didn't turn after 1990 and right now there are fewer than 100,000 breeding pairs in the Netherlands. Since my adolescence we have lost 80% of our House Martins. This does not mean that House Martins are close to extinction. It just means that people in towns and in most villages must miss seeing them.

Why are there far fewer House Martins than three decades ago? What do these House Martins tell us about our environment? Should we worry about these issues? Is there any connection between the gains in geese and the losses of House Martins? We will get to that in a minute, but let's first examine the plight of British House Martins in some more detail.

Alarm at the Oxford bridges

Remember ploughman Derek Warren from Suffolk whom we met in the story on 'Birds of happiness'? In the mid-1960s he said: "*There were always the martins. Each house seems to have so many people in it and so many martins.*" This is now an unthinkable situation. In Suffolk, as elsewhere in the English countryside, houses with House Martin nests are a major rarity.

Though the UK can take pride in having the best quantitative information on the numbers and distribution of birds (and some other groups of organisms), any interpretation of changes in numbers suffers from the 'shifting baseline syndrome', caused by necessarily using quite recent counts as reference points to evaluate the well-being of current populations. The shifting baseline syndrome can be seen as a loss of perception, each generation redefining what is 'natural'. It underestimates the extent of change, and worse, it may hinder the correct identification of the drivers of change. On the basis of country wide quantitative information on bird numbers that started in the 1960s, the British Trust for Ornithology now reports that over the last 50 years House Martins have declined by about two-thirds. Does Warren's remark suggest that (over a slightly expanded time frame), the losses could actually have been much greater?

M.C. Radford was a medical doctor with strong bird interests who, in her eighties, worked in the Alexander Library of the Edward Grey Institute of Ornithology in Oxford in the days when the young ornithologists Ian Newton and Chris Perrins were studying under David Lack, assembling their respective DPhil theses. In 1966 she published *The Birds of Berkshire and Oxfordshire*, in which she gives figures for the number of House Martin nests on two stone bridges over the River Thames near Oxford. Both bridges are quite ancient, and are situated in the countryside at Swinford near Eynsham (seven kilometres northwest of Oxford) and near Clifton Hampden (11 kilometres south of Oxford). W.B. Alexander, after whom the ornithological library is named, was actually one of the people involved in the proper counting of the House Martin nests under the bridges. There is a photo of a greying Alexander in swimsuit, wading with a stick across the river towards the bridge at Clifton Hampden, looking up in great anticipation.

For the Clifton Hampden bridge, Dr Radford reported 400–500 House Martin nests in the early 1950s. This dipped towards 100 nests around 1960, by which time the Radford series was continued by figures in the annual Oxford Bird Reports. Numbers increased again towards 300 nests in the mid-1960s. This was followed by a sudden decline from 192 counted nests in 1966 to zero in 1967, but things picked up again, with 103 nests counted in 1975. However, this partial recovery was followed by a terminal decline to four nests in 1981, with none reported since.

The Swinford/Eynsham bridge was counted first in 1959, when it had 80 nests. Numbers varied yearly between 70 and 140 occupied nests until 1971, after which numbers steeply declined. The last positive count at Swinford was 12 House Martin nests in 1980.

To this day both bridges offer beautiful potential nest locations in seemingly idyllic landscapes (I used Google Street View to examine the situation, and tried to take the perspective of a House Martin), but the bridges have been deserted since 1981. If we take Radford's counts at Clifton Hampden as a cue, relative to the early 1950s numbers were down by at least half by the time the BTO assembled its first House Martin population estimate in the 1960s. Using this for extrapolation, it would mean that since World War II the UK lost 84% of its House

Martins (a sixfold decline), rather than 67% (a threefold decline, still good enough for a recent 'amber' listing in the UK). Still, Warren's comment for Suffolk, together with the total disappearance of House Martins from the two Oxford bridges, suggest that the real trajectory of decline may have been even steeper. It may also have started earlier.

As a remedy to the shifting baseline syndrome, it would have been fantastic if the Reverend Gilbert White had been as quantitatively inclined as he was an astute observer of bird behaviour and processes in nature. What we do know is that House Martins have all but disappeared from Selborne now. The house of Robert Saltmarsh in Gracious Street had 11 House Martin nests in 1965, one in 2008, and none since.

Elsewhere in Hampshire House Martins have fared little better. In 2000 my wader-watching friend Pete Potts carried out a community project in the parish of Bishops Waltham, 25 kilometres southwest of Selborne. Among 3,500 homes, he found only two with small colonies and a few houses with single nests. The presence of House Martin nests at no more than one fifth of a percent of the houses in a nice part of rural England sounds very different from 'each house having both people and House Martins'.

There actually is quantitative evidence of a near-total loss of nesting House Martins, even with baseline observations starting as recently as 1980, in all parts of Hampshire. Colonies in the suburbs of Portsmouth had House Martin nests then, but they have all long gone. The old vicarage next to the White Horse pub at Soberton, even as late as 1993, had 60 nests, but not a single pair is left there today. It was in this area that the father and son team, Theo and Graham Roberts, who had House Martins nesting on their own house, took to catching and ringing breeding birds and their chicks in 1973. They ringed c 1,200 House Martins over the ensuing two decades, but very few after 1986; they stopped their efforts in 1993!

A more 'integrated', albeit a less 'quantitative' signal of House Martin losses comes from observations of their autumn passage in coastal Hampshire. This occurs from late August into October, with peaks between mid-September and early October in most years. Pete Potts, Graham Roberts, Richard Levett and others recall that in the 1980s numbers were very large. They remember 'uncountable' concentrations of House Martins gathering and lingering on the coast, especially in 1981. It is nothing like that any more.

A fresh jewel in the crown of British and Irish ornithology was the *Bird Atlas 2007–11* published in 2013. The atlas shows maps of the changes in breeding range and abundance for most birds across Britain and Ireland over the last 20 years. The map for House Martins confirms that across much of England, and especially in the south-east, between 1990 and 2010 House Martins kept on declining. At the same time there were increases in parts of Scotland and Ireland.

A north-west to south-east gradient of increasing declines across the British Isles was evident also in the map for Sand Martins and to a lesser degree the maps for Barn Swallow and Swift (the latter two species showed the most widespread declines). That four swallow-like species with rather different wintering areas and ecologies show such congruent population trends suggests that any common cause for the gradient could be local to the UK. The geographical gradient from north-west to south-east is a fit to the gradient of increasing extents of arable farming and pesticide use (or a decrease in the extent of grassland pasture). Although grasslands have become very uniform and intensive all across the lowlands of Britain and Ireland, increased tree planting in north and west Britain and in Ireland across this period may have resulted in more insects, especially aphids, in the air column.

Countryside detectives

Since meeting percussionist, composer and birdwatcher Sytze Pruiksma almost ten years ago, we've shared a love for mudflats, open countryside, and the birds that live there. We continually look for cross-pollinations between his artistic and my scientific worlds.

Together with singer Nynke Laverman, Sytze lives on the edge of the village of Weidum, so from their living room they look across the sweeping pastureland of central Friesland, but unfortunately the meadows consist of English ryegrass only; flowers are absent. In 2013, ditch dredgings were dumped on one of the fields near their house and it was here, in the course of the summer, that amid the green monotony, a splash of camomile appeared. A sea of flowers! Sytze immediately noticed that Barn Swallows and House Martins only hunted for food over this camomile, completely ignoring the newly cut ryegrass.

Intensive farming practices developed in Britain during World War II when the country was cut off from its economic partners and had to rely on its own agricultural production. By the end of the war people in the Netherlands, as well as in other parts of mainland Europe, really starved. That was never to happen again, and within a slowly establishing and growing European community, policies sharply focused on helping the growth of food production.

Humankind had just learned how to make fertilisers from nitrogen derived from air, apparently accepting that binding atmospheric nitrogen is an energy-slurping process. With lots of oil and new technologies at our disposal, there seemed to be no limits, though it took some time for the process to gain momentum and it was not until the 1970s and 1980s that the process of agricultural industrialisation really took off.

The countryside of the UK and the Netherlands was bulldozed, water tables were contained and strictly regulated at much lower levels than before. Small-scale patchworks of meadows were replaced by immense but dull, dry fields with ryegrass and cereal crops. In consequence, more than 95% of all wet flower-rich meadows disappeared, the remainder being negatively affected by loss of water along the edges and spillovers of pesticide from the surrounding area. These changes were not limited to the UK and the Netherlands of course, with most of western Europe and much of temperate North America following suit. Today this suffocating blanket of land 'improvements' combined with man-made fertilisers, herbicides and insecticides is still spreading across eastern Europe and vast parts of Asia, Africa, and Latin America, obliterating biodiversity in its march. Even the mighty landscapes of Iceland now suffer from this cause.

House Martins need insects. Insects need flowers for feeding. This could well be the whole story explaining the presence of martins and swallows over Sytze's camomile patch, but it isn't. The more that fields get ploughed, the fewer insect larvae survive because the insects simply don't get enough time to successfully complete their life cycle. On top of this, increased fertilisation results in smaller insects: the larvae of larger insects living in the soil are pushed out of the business of recycling natural nutrients, because nutrients supplied as artificial fertiliser and liquid manure are instantly available for growing grass and other crops. Nutrients no longer need releasing from solid manure and other organic material by an army of soil-dwelling decomposers.

Butterflies and grasshoppers have totally disappeared from the Dutch meadows, even though not long ago creatures like cockchafers (or May bugs) were considered pests in our place. I even don't know the animal, I just know the word 'May bug'. The extinction of larger types of insects in agricultural areas has contributed to the virtual disappearance of breeding Skylarks from the rural parts of the Netherlands, and strong declines in the breeding populations of Lapwings (with a loss of 85%), Black-tailed Godwits (80% gone), along with many other bird species.

The decline of the flying arthropods that feed the House Martins, the Swifts and the Barn Swallows, the so-called 'aeroplankton', was documented directly in the UK. This involved an array of large vacuum cleaners developed at the world-famous arable crops research centre at Rothamsted that in standardised ways suck up aeroplankton. Initially biologists were mainly interested in potential insect pests such as the aphids that each spring would drift into England on easterly and south-easterly winds. Aphids have the tendency to become pests on many types of vegetable plants, so in order to register their arrival and numbers of aphids – as if it were the weather forecast – 12-metre-high pipes were installed. On top of each pipe sat a large funnel which sucked up all insects and spiders that flew or drifted in range.

The Rothamsted Hoovers showed that across the UK the mass of insect aeroplankton declined between 1970 and 2005. Not surprisingly, the numbers of insectivorous birds were correlated with the weight of the aeroplankton. But two findings stand out for me. Firstly, the drop in the number of insects was greatest in those areas where agricultural intensification was highest. Secondly, the largest reduction in insects occurred within the black flies Bibionidae, which are top of the House Martin menu. Therefore, the use of artificial fertiliser and liquid manure, drainage, and the sowing of just ryegrass and cereals, marked the end of flowers and many insects. And in the wake of this, we observe the disappearance of the birds that depend on them.

The great importance of insect aeroplankton to breeding House Martins was best demonstrated in experimental research in the Rhône delta of southern France. This area, the Camargue, is known for its white horses and the gipsies of Saintes-Maries-de-la-Mer. If you ever went there for a holiday, you may well remember the number of mosquito bites you suffered, because in summer the warm marshland-waters swarm with mosquitos. Locals suffer just as much as the tourists, which is why they spray against these moustiques, using a 'green' poison that is called Bti. This material contains bacteria that produce proteins which are poisonous to mosquito larvae. So, it is not too awkward a chemical. Spray the larvae-rich waters with Bti and the mosquito larvae will die.

Biologists compared the diet and the breeding success of House Martins in sprayed and unsprayed areas. In the unsprayed areas House Martins mainly ate mosquitos. In the sprayed areas they fed on the only alternative – flying ants. In areas that were free of mosquitos, House Martins laid one fewer egg. On average only two chicks were raised instead of three.

Without these nasty moustiques the House Martins of the Camargue no longer raised enough young to maintain their numbers. In a situation like this, declines are rapid. A similar loss of insects seemed to have happened across the Netherlands and in the UK between 1980 and 1990. What puzzles me is that so often the loss of House Martins is attributed to the loss of suitable nesting places with many new houses having plastic fascias under their eaves, making them less suitable for nesting House Martins. But the Oxfordshire bridges and the Hampshire pubs that gave space to hundreds of nests half a century ago are still perfectly ready to receive them again, so something else must be amiss. What a shame that no one really kept track of House Martin reproduction, or House Martin diets, or, in places like the Netherlands, the richness of the aeroplankton that swallow-like species feed on; that hardly anyone was watching. We just seem to have let it happen, our collective sight on the matter additionally blurred by the shifting baseline syndrome.

Now and again there is someone who is quick to see the big picture and who sounds the alarm. Such messages are usually, and conveniently, ignored. *Silent Spring* by Rachel Carson was a big exception. In the early 1960s her book managed to make a substantial difference and led eventually to the abolition of DDT and other organochlorine pesticides. In the meantime new problematic chemicals have come on the market, such as the neonicotinoids that since the mid-1990s have seen a steep rise in popularity.

Neonicotinoids are synthetic variants of nicotine that damage the nervous system of insects even in tiny amounts. Applied as seed dressings before crops are sown (and, as we now know, with huge leakage to the soil), the insecticide spreads through the growing plant, killing any insect that tries to feed on it. Neonicotinoids have become one of the most abundantly used classes of agrochemical in the world, with the British and Dutch governments insisting for as long as they can that they are ecologically safe.

However, the emerging truth is different. Neonicotinoids are far from safe. The evidence of them being responsible for disoriented honeybees and bumblebees, disappearing insects of all kinds, and now even the birds that feed on these insects, is rapidly mounting. Moreover, like DDT, they are persistent and don't break down readily. In fact, neonicotinoids have already been proclaimed as 'the new DDT, killing the natural world'. Carson could certainly not have anticipated that our springs, even without DDT, would become as silent as they have.

In the summer of 2014, Ian Newton visited El Rocio, a village of pilgrimage in the heart of the Doñana, that famous and vast seasonal wetland in Andalucia, Spain. On a pilgrimage of an ornithological kind, he was struck by the great numbers of House Martins nesting in El Rocio. As it happens, Petra and I were there later in the year and we were similarly impressed, especially by the fantastic numbers of nests on the white walls below the eaves of Puente del Rey, a large building dominating the sandy entrance to the village. The orange-brown clays used by the House Martins beautifully mirrored the colours in the tiled roof. I counted 925 nests (mostly intact, but some already crumbled down to the base), perhaps a baseline figure in the years to come. El Rocio embodies the soul of Doñana, but is also home to an extensive and still growing strawberry industry. Neonicotinoids are widely used in this business, thus adding insult to injury (the depletion of the groundwater in this wetland ecosystem). Yes, you have correctly surmised that I am concerned about the future of the magnificent House Martin colony of El Rocio.

Athletes in poverty

It has become very green in our farmland, but it also has become very quiet. In my dreams about the world before the agricultural industrialisation, I imagine how in spring and summer flying insects rose out of all meadows, much as ants still do from a sandy corner of the garden at the end of a hot summer day. Flying ants attract your attention because House Sparrows, House Martins, Barn Swallows, and Black-headed Gulls hunt for them over the village. I also imagine how large numbers of meadow birds, Swifts and hirundines managed to live comfortably on these insects. How lively and rich the countryside was only a generation ago.

In his book *Expeditie Wildernis* (2012), Bram van der Klundert describes a couple of days in September spent at Bargerveen, one of the last remaining Dutch peatlands situated on the German border. Over a small wet area he spotted an abundance of House Martins: *"I never saw Barn Swallows and House Martins in such quantities, and certainly not House Martins. Over the peat pools thousands of them foraged frantically for as many insects as they could catch before the long journey. Over the adjacent arable land not a single bird was to be seen. The contrast between agriculture and nature is moving towards extremes. It is obvious to all of us that in a glasshouse only those crops appear which the owner intends to grow there, but this form of absolute monoculture is gradually becoming the norm of arable land, and even of pastures."* He continues gloomily for a while and concludes that, "*Farmers seem to demand a nature-free environment.*"

The research of David Bryant shows that House Martins work hardest in the weeks when the fast-growing chicks have to be fed. Even during fine-weather days House Martins slave away from sunrise till sunset. Although they glide a lot – waiting for an insect to pass by – the hunt for moving flies is an expensive activity. When caring for their chicks, House Martins work as hard as professional racing cyclists in the Tour de France. And they have to keep it up for longer too.

Swifts

I've been seriously in love with an individual bird only once. It was a young Swift that was found on the street by a colleague one summer day. This happens regularly and these young birds can quite easily be rescued by feeding them pellets of minced meat. After a week to a fortnight you can throw them as high as possible into the air from where they usually keep flying. However, this bird had a wing defect and therefore it was still living with my Bavarian friend into the winter.

What a delightful bird it was! She had big dark beady eyes on either side of her broad beak. These eyes probingly gazed at you and really made contact. She lived on an old woollen jersey in a cardboard box – the colleague was of the jersey-wearing type. When it was time for a chat or a pellet of meat, she would crawl up a sleeve and once she'd reached the shoulder she would make her presence known by begging for attention. I have forgotten her name. She died, later that winter.

One and a half years later, on 6 July, a young Swift was brought to me by Johan Hoekstra from his farm where it had fallen from high under the roof into an empty hay compartment. It had fledged too early, I think, for the bird was rather small and light and couldn't fly at all. With the Bavarian Swift in mind, I of course immediately took care of this young bird. We called him Jappy, and Jappy stayed with us for three and a half weeks. But Jappy was very different from the lovely Swift I had met before. Jappy avoided us completely, did not make any contact at all, and threw up his pellets of minced meat with mealworms as often as possible. Because of this, feeding became a true struggle – eight times a day.

Jappy weighed 28.2 grams when Johan brought him in; despite all the minced meat his weight soon dropped to 25.6 grams. He was an ungrateful guest, even though we always had to be home or find a bird-sitter. But his wings did grow: from 115 millimetres on 6 July to 156 millimetres on 1 August, the day Petra and I released him, weighing 31.9 grams. This is approximately ten grams below the weight of incubating parent Swifts.

That he wanted to remain quite light is understandable. Less weight makes flying easier. In fact, such weight-loss before they leave the nest occurs in all young Swifts – and as we have seen it applies to House Martin chicks too. It has been suggested that Swifts do push-ups under the roof tiles to make sure that they are light enough to fledge. At fledging everything must be right, otherwise you end up in an empty hay loft or in somebody's garden. Jappy did what is most important to a Swift: he let his wings grow.

The day before his release we did a practice run in the largest room of the house. After short fluttering of wings and ending up in the curtains, we thought he showed progress. On the lovely first day of August we took the stepladder into the fields behind the village. The plan was to stand on the highest rung and throw Jappy into the air as high as possible. It worked. Jappy made a few uncertain wingbeats, and off he went! He made one lap around the field and on to the village – where he teamed up with some other Swifts. From that moment on Jappy was anonymous again, but you may not be surprised that we still talk about him.

Just as people believe that they are the pinnacle of creation – because we humans have such powerful brains – Swifts for sure look at themselves in similar ways. After all, there is no bird that can fly as long or as well as they can. In Latin Swifts are called Apodidae, the feetless, because in ancient times wise men believed that Swifts did not have legs at all. Swifts are the icon of all flyers, they represent the ultimate bird. They fly so well and so much that they can do without legs. However, their eggs cannot fly, so they need a secure place to incubate them, whether under a tile, against a wall or on a branch. To do this Swifts need grip. Strong long toes are what Swifts rely on leg-wise.

Besides the incubation of eggs and the feeding of their chicks, Swifts do everything in the air. Here they eat, sleep, and mate. I have seen this mid-air mating a couple of times, always in May. Two Swifts that seem to fall from the sky attached to one another with their tails; it is immediately clear that something out of the ordinary is going on. Suddenly they then let go and fly off, accelerating and climbing.

Just like House Martins they chase for insects high in the air. Although they have light-coloured throats, Swifts do not look like orcas; a comparison with false killer whale seems more appropriate. However, the Alpine Swifts that live in the mountains of southern Europe do have the black-and-white counter-shading of orcas.

In spring, Swifts don't arrive until fairly late – late April/early May – and leave early also, by the end of July. By not building nests, they save time and never breed more than once per summer. In that small hollow space underneath a roof they raise one, two or three chicks, whereas House Martins raise four to eight in a summer. Swifts can afford small families because they survive better than House Martins. In fact, Swifts, which on average live around ten years, don't start breeding until they are two or three years old, whereas House Martins only live for about three years.

Similar to House Martins, their winter destinations remained a mystery. However, due to their habit of accepting nest boxes – which makes them easy to capture multiple times – and because Swifts are larger than House Martins and able to carry small electronic tracking devices, in 2012 their winter locations were discovered and could be published...

Migration secrets revealed

Lund is a small town in Skåne, the southernmost province of Sweden, a province that was under Danish rule for a long time. Apart from King Canute's cathedral and the TetraPak headquarters (the developers and producers of the square milk and fruit juice cartons), Lund has a large university where many biologists work on bird migration. It makes sense that the study of bird migration should flourish in the south of Sweden, because a major migration route lies near Lund. Migratory birds and the stories about them are a source of inspiration for scientists, but also for writers.

The most famous by far is Selma Lagerlöf (1858–1940) who received the Nobel Prize for Literature in 1909 and who achieved great renown for her stories of Nils Holgersson. Nils is the farmer's son from Skåne, the boy who'd always been a bad lot and who was turned by magic into a gnome. On the back of a goose Nils undertakes an adventurous journey to the north of Sweden and back home again. He experiences this trip and his country from a migratory bird's perspective. Selma Lagerlöf, who was paralysed and unable to walk, managed to place herself extremely well in the position of birds. The moral of the story shows Nils's transformation from a little rotter into an agreeable lad. And finally he changes from a gnome into a boy again.

One of the finest and most modest scientists I know, the agreeable Nils Holgersson of our time, is Thomas Alerstam. He is a professor in animal ecology at the University of Lund and grew up in Skåne – just like Lagerlöf and Holgersson. Since childhood he has been inspired by bird migration and he has carried out research on 'birds on the move' ever since the late 1960s.

Thomas uses all types of methods to solve the secrets of bird migration, but his speciality is the use of radar. As a student he laid hands on old military radar equipment and carried out hugely innovative research with it. Nowadays, such a device stands on top of the university's new Ecology Building. From this Ekologihuset, Thomas and his students can study birds on the move – often birds that come from the Netherlands. In early May the last remaining Ruffs staging in the Netherlands fly over Lund; in late May and early June the Bar-tailed Godwits and Red Knots follow, on their way from the Wadden Sea to the Siberian tundra. Thomas has many scientific offspring, most of whom managed to find research jobs at the university. I am happy to be one of his 'offspring' too; well, more or less.

Friends in Alerstam's team caught Swifts in nest boxes and attached so-called geolocators on their backs. These instruments weigh only one gram so don't bother the Swifts, which weigh 40 grams themselves. Geolocators consist of a light meter, a clock, and a chip to record the intensity of the light once a minute. All locations on earth have their own cycle of light and darkness. If you register these times with the help of a very accurate clock, it is possible to calculate where a specific geolocator on a bird hangs out. Such estimates are not very accurate, of course, with a deviation of a few hundred kilometres, but they enabled researchers to check whether the Swifts were in Skåne or whether they reached the south of Germany, Spain, Morocco, Mali, Nigeria or Congo. This sequence of places actually describes their journey towards the wintering area.

Most Swifts from southern Sweden were shown to fly across Europe in a south-westerly direction, crossing to Africa via Gibraltar before flying south over the Sahara, turned left at Senegal, and kept going towards the east once south of the Sahel. They then turned right above

Chad and continued south into the Congo. Here they arrived in early October and stayed all winter. For at least six months they kept flying above the remains of the rainforests of Congo, Cameroon, and Gabon. Every single day, according to the geolocators, the birds were constantly on the move, in darkness or in the light. This means that Swifts never went down into the semi-darkness of the rainforest but slept and ate in the African sky for the entire winter period.

Only as April draws to an end do the Swedish Swifts with geolocators start their journey north. It takes them precisely one month and what a journey it is! First they fly north-east and cross the Guinean Gulf, straight for the Liberian forests. Here they hang out for a week to gain weight, to store enough fat to fuel a non-stop flight across the Sahara and the Mediterranean, and all of Europe as well, averaging 500 kilometres a day. Then, sometime in May, the Swifts were recaptured in their nest boxes in Skåne. They had not only survived their journeys, they returned with answers to secrets tied to their backs. Thomas Alerstam's people buckled down to the geolocator data, and so they were the first to get the story of the 21st-century reincarnation of Nils Holgersson.

As the Swedish Swifts with geolocators returned to Skåne in the early summer of 2010, researchers in the UK and the Netherlands were busy with geolocators during the summers of 2010 and 2011 and when birds returned with their secrets in 2011 and 2012 it was apparent that both British and Dutch breeding Swifts carry out even more phenomenal migrations than the Swedish birds!

Whereas the Swedes winter above the central African rainforests, the Brits and the Dutch make an additional journey as far as the Indian Ocean. Extending the migration with another 5,000-kilometre return trip, they follow the rains to spend much of December and January above the forested parts of Malawi and north Mozambique before returning to Congo. In addition, British and Dutch Swifts distinguished themselves from the Swedes in scheduling both their northward and southward migrations two weeks earlier.

I am not that fond of forests myself. The disadvantage of trees undoubtedly is that they take away one's view of the forest. With Swifts staying above rainforest most of the winter, it explains why they are hardly ever seen in Africa. And because they are not seen, we have no idea what they eat or what they do. Some think that in Congo they concentrate on flying termites which ascend en masse during rain showers. Something similar has been described for the forests in Liberia. Termites fly here in the second half of April, just as the Swifts have arrived from Congo.

Rob Bijlsma did see Swifts in Africa. Twice. Here is what Rob saw, in his own words: "*Swifts may turn up in gigantic numbers everywhere after thunderstorms and rain, and disappear just as quickly. As evening approached on January 18, 1995, during our Barn Swallow adventures in Botswana we saw more than 10,000 Swifts rush by, madly snapping termites from the sky, termites which had come out after the downpour. Or that other time near Kintampo in Ghana, when we were taken by surprise in the early morning of March 7, 2011, by compact, screeching balls of 390 and then 100 Swifts which twirled sky-high like mosquitoes and disappeared within minutes towards the south.*"

It is almost unthinkable, says Rob, to have such sightings of House Martins. Not because there aren't any House Martins there, but because they are so much smaller and fly even higher than Swifts. On top of all that, their sound is much more modest. "*It won't be easy to find these specks against the clear blue sky, or even worse: during the harmattan, the periods with dry dusty winds from the north, when even the sun is nothing but a veiled orange ball in a dusty sky.*"

To the Congo too?

I cried while reading David Van Reybrouck's authoritative history of Congo. What suffering, what abuse of power! All these coups, each time followed by new massacres and the large-scale destruction of culture and nature. During Belgian colonial rule things were rough, but afterwards the people of Congo were far worse off.

Van Reybrouck starts with a description of the River Congo. After almost 5,000 kilometres, this mighty stream thrusts its way through a small opening in the coastal cliffs and out into the Atlantic. Geology ensures this river is not allowed the time or the space to form a beautiful delta such as those of the Nile or the Rhine. Horatio Clare travelled through Congo as he followed the migration of Barn Swallows from South Africa north to Wales. During this journey he visits the cascades, the rapids just before the River Congo leaves the African continent. The water moves with thundering vigour, around 40,000 cubic metres of water per second. Wild waves everywhere and water bursting, fountains of at least ten metres high, and among all this: Barn Swallows! Clare states that it took his breath away when he saw the first Swallow escaping from this churning and bursting water. When the water came too close, the Barn Swallows slipped past effortlessly on their sides. House Martins would not go that close to the river's turmoil; they would keep their distance. But would Clare have been able to find them there, lying on his back, staring at the sky?

Given that House Martins are so similar to Swifts in looking for aeroplanktonic food items high up in the sky, and perhaps also sleeping up there just like Swifts; given that House Martins are seen less frequently than Swifts away from the Eurasian breeding grounds; couldn't they be doing exactly the same as Swifts during winter? Of the one million House Martins ringed in Europe during the last century, only 21 generated a response from Africa south of the Sahara. Of course this proves that they do cross the mighty desert, but the remainder of Africa is so huge.

The 21 responses also taught us that House Martins ringed in western or eastern Europe would be respectively recovered in western or eastern Africa too. In technical slang it says that breeding and non-breeding longitudes are strongly correlated. For the House Martins of Gaast this would mean that they'd winter somewhere on the north–south axis across Niger/Cameroon/Gabon/Angola. A little west of the Congo rainforest, but is it in the Sahel, the savannah regions, or the rainforest?

Because House Martins are too small to carry a geolocator on their back (and note that a backpack may be quite a hindrance when squeezing through the entrance hole into their nest), we looked for different methods to uncover their secrets. The slogan 'You are what you eat' became the centre of the detective-work that I started together with Keith Hobson, Steven van Wilgenburg and Len Wassenaar. These men are employed by a governmental institute for the environment in Saskatchewan, on the prairies of western Canada. Keith is an English expat who fell in love with House Martins at a tender young age. Steven carries a Dutch surname and Len would have been called Lieuwe, had his parents not emigrated from Bitgum in Friesland to Canada. It was easy to make Len happy with *Cruel Paradise: Life Stories of Dutch Emigrants* of the Frisian writer Hylke Speerstra.

What makes these three men so special is that they belong to the world's top isotope scientists while carrying a deep interest in ornithology. Isotopes are varieties of atoms that are distinct from the common forms by a different number of neutrons. Chemically speaking the different isotopes of one element function the same way, but they differ in relative weight because of physical principles – one extra neutron gives an atom just a fraction more weight.

The heavier atoms, be it hydrogen, carbon, or nitrogen, are rare and their occurrences vary in space and time. The presence of the heavy hydrogen isotope is related to the kind of rain that falls on the land; carbon varies with the type of plants that grow somewhere; and in the case of nitrogen the presence of the heavy isotope is correlated with the degree of use of artificial fertiliser. Plants consist of water – with a minuscule bit of the heavy hydrogen atoms – and of carbon and nitrogen. Plants get eaten by insects, and insects by House Martins, so in principle you can see what and where the birds collected their food by looking at the isotopic 'fingerprints' in tissues, such as blood or feathers, produced at the time.

Keith, Steven, and Len have charted the regional differences in isotope concentrations across Africa. If we could manage to analyse House Martin tissue produced in Africa, we could compare the resulting fingerprint with the isotope chart made by the men from Saskatchewan.

Feathers experience wear and tear and birds replace all of them at least once a year. We know that House Martins don't replace the long feathers of the wing during their summers with us and because missing wing feathers are best avoided during migration, we suspect House Martins replace the wing feathers in winter, as do Barn Swallows and Swifts. Thus, if we collected some wing-feather material from House Martins in Gaast, we should be able to determine which African regions best match the isotope profile of the feathers. Fortunately, the mass spectrometers that do the profiling can work with tiny amounts of material: a few milligrams will do. Two small feather tips was all I needed from the House Martins, which everyone agreed would be a trivial loss to the birds.

I faithfully sent feather tips to Saskatchewan for four consecutive summers. After the lab work was done, Steven played the part of clever calculator. Testing a basic assumption, we could show that the isotopic profiles of feathers of recently fledged House Martins were substantially different from those of adult birds. The former were built out of insects collected in the Frisian airspace. The feather tips of adult House Martins clearly showed isotopic profiles indicating tropical rainforests, which suggest that the Gaast martins winter in… Cameroon and Congo!

Epilogue: travel companions

In April 1988 I was working on the African counterpart of the Wadden Sea, a magnificent coastal area in Mauritania, a place where the Sahara meets the Atlantic Ocean, called Banc d'Arguin. We were there to investigate the conditions which triggered the northward migration of the waders we knew so well from the Wadden Sea. We studied their rise in body weight and their departures – on what type of days and at what time.

Bar-tailed Godwits, Red Knots and the other shorebirds always left at the end of the day. Late in the afternoon but well before sunset they assembled in nervous, noisy, restless flocks. Then there would come a moment that part of the flock, 50 birds perhaps, or 100, would take to the air. Gradually climbing against the northern trade winds they would disappear from sight. We now know that after departure these birds keep flying for three full days and nights until arrival in the Wadden Sea. Unlike hirundines and other songbirds, these shorebirds don't take travel breaks. Even during journeys that last several days, they don't seem to sleep.

Of course we needed to sleep and on the Banc d'Arguin we did so in tents. Large frame tents served as a kitchen and an office. Some evenings around sunset one or two Barn Swallows would shoot in and perch on a pile of books; away from the wind and in the shelter of the tent they spent the night sleeping there. The fact that humans also made use of these tents didn't bother them. In terms of a safe place for the night we obviously had more to offer than the entire desert around us. At the start of a new day the birds would leave the tent. On the boundary of desert and ocean, while negotiating headwinds and occasionally snapping up a little fly, they continued the long journey north.

Since helping to discover that the House Martins of Gaast travel to Cameroon and Congo and spend more than half a year in the skies above their forests and fields, I have wondered what goes on there. If these birds really remain in the air all the time (high up in the cold, where the feathers insulating their legs would make a difference), how is it possible that we find them harbouring malarial blood parasites? Do the African mosquitoes fly high as well, or do Hobbies, which also migrate to the Congo rainforests, occasionally chase them into the trees? Do House Martins get bitten by malaria-carrying mosquitoes while finding safety in treetops?

How close can you get to the essence of a bird? How well can human beings place themselves in the position of flying creatures with the weight of fountain pens? Some philosophers have said that it is downright impossible to know what it is like to be an(other) animal. Like the British author Horatio Clare and the Dutch bird painter Erik van Ommen, one can travel in the company of Barn Swallows, but it is a human voyage, not a bird voyage.

I think I understand the argument of these philosophers, but I also think that they are perhaps a little too lazy, or at least not enough of a biologist, to truly connect to another animal's life. I believe it is actually even easier to know what it is like to be a Barn Swallow than a Swift or a House Martin. This is because Barn Swallows sleep in reed beds or elephant grass (and tents!); because they breed in barns and stables near humans; because they fly just above the ground. This seems easier than putting yourself in the position of the high-flying and more aerobatic aviators.

Since House Martins are capable of putting themselves in our shoes when assessing the threat to their nests, why couldn't we think a bit like a House Martin?

Acknowledgements

That there would ever be an edition in one of the world's biggest languages, English, of a little book written in what comes close to its ancestral language, yet one of the world's smallest, Frisian, has a lot to do with four English friends: Nicola Crockford, Rodney West, Margaret Grenham and Ian Newton. Nicola pushed the ball and made sure it kept rolling, Rodney and Maggie, time and again, were sources of knowledge and inspiration both with respect to the swallow-like species, and with respect to historical connections between Friesland and East Anglia.

It almost seems an accident of history that the four of us can now embody the back-and-forths across the southern North Sea made by the Old-English/Old-Frisians, albeit by air between Amsterdam and Norwich rather than by sailing boat between Wynaam and Iken. Ian's immediate and sustained interests gave me the confidence that a translation could work, and all four of them have contributed a great deal by their early reading, reflections and edits.

As far as I know everything in this book is true, except for the first chapter. Jacob de Groot does go out with a metal detector regularly and he has found quite a lot of old coins around Gaast, as well as two bird rings. But these were not of House Martins. The rings are made of aluminium, and I am not even sure that a metal detector would be able to find them. At this point I chose to exercise my artistic licence.

Lammert and Karin Miedema have nesting House Martins on their house, and I have regularly recaptured 'their' martins after one, two, or three years.

I probably got my inspiration for writing the present account from a book that dates back from before my birth. In *Swifts in a Tower*, published in 1956, the English ornithologist David Lack unpretentiously, and with as much entertainment value as an episode of the television series Inspector Morse, tells how he tried to solve the mysteries of the Swifts of Oxford. His book also provided me with the story about the 13th-century man who tied a note to a Swallow's leg with the question about where the bird stayed in winter.

David Winkler of Cornell University in Ithaca, New York, is a friend and his swallow-mania has been contagious. Information about the centuries-long discussions about the whereabouts of swallows and martins, and whether or not swallows hibernate in the mud, came from another friend, Thomas Alerstam from Lund in Sweden. I took the concept of understanding mysteries and their beauty from an article by my colleague Gerrit Breeuwsma published in the Groningen University Newspaper (UK) on 27 May 2010.

Usually Rob Bijlsma can be found in the woods of the Dutch province of Drenthe; from there and for many years he has been a tremendous source of inspiration. He was the one who gave me the book on swallows by E.A. Lind. I was most grateful that Keith Hobson, Steven van Wilgenburg and Len Wassenaar got on board my House Martin project, and that we were able to deliver successfully. Marco van der Velde is a true DNA artist with whom it is a pleasure to work.

Jan van Dijk, the former skipper of the State Forest Service's survey vessel 'Phoca', and I have been through a lot over the past 20 years: on the coastal mudflats of course; as his neighbour in Oosterend on the isle of Texel; but also on many expeditions in Mauritania. Jan has a crush on Barn Swallows and he counts the ones in Oosterend. Every summer for many years he came across the Afsluitdijk to Gaast for the annual 24-hour ringing spree. Jan-with-the-net has become part of the summer imagery of our village.

I would also like to thank the inhabitants of the houses with House Martin nests for their tolerance of the birds, their poo and our breaching their privacy each summer: Gosse de Groot and his family, Lammert and Karin, Elwin and Sinny, Fokke and Ulkje, and (the late) Thom and his Ruurdtsje. In 2005 Joop Jukema got me started on catching and ringing; after that Petra de Goeij helped me numerous times.

Others helped with the catching too: Allan Baker, Pierrick Bocher, Eelco Brandenburg, Allert Bijleveld, Ysbrand Galama, Margaret Grenham, Barbara Jonkers, Roos Kentie, Pedro Lourenço, Kim Mathot, Yaa Ntiamoa-Baidu, Lucie Schmaltz, Sybrecht Speerstra, Klaas Sietse and Suze Rixt Spoelstra, Steven Sterk, Sytze Pruiksma, Fred Robin, Irene Tieleman, Marco van der Velde, Mo Verhoeven, Elwin and Sinny de Vink, Rodney West, and Jan Wijmenga.

The Vogeltrekstation Arnhem represented by Gert Speek and Henk van der Jeugd, together with Richard Ubels and Jos Hooijmeijer of the University of Groningen, assisted with the practical and administrative side of the endeavour. Roos Kentie looked after the House Martin survival calculations.

Eelco Brandenburg is cheeky enough to stroll through people's gardens without asking. Over many summers he has kept track of the well-being of the House Martin populations in villages in south-west Friesland. Eelco was always prepared to share the latest news. I thank Gerrit Twijnstra for the story of the 'hanged martin' of It Heidenskip and photographs documenting it. Klaas Ybema, the weather-man of Workum, helped me access meteorological information from the Schettens weather station, to see if the weal and woe of the House Martins in Gaast would be connected to weather (they were).

Marten Sikkema shared a childhood story, and Hannes Scherjon told about his father Eelke. The story of the swallows and martins above the camomile field in Weidum comes from Sytze Pruiksma. I am most grateful for Nynke Laverman's translation into Frisian of a section of Macbeth. Frits van Oostrom and Ingrid Biesheuvel helped me with notations of various words for 'Swallow' in Middle Dutch and a variety of old sayings.

Angela Turner helped find an unpublished PhD thesis (the one by D.R. Waugh). Jason Chapman provided me with literature on the Rothamsted insect survey. Ruud van Beusekom spontaneously left me a small German book on House Martins. Rodney West and Margaret Grenham taught me what it's like to hold a Sand Martin. Johan van de Gronden offered insightful remarks on the Dutch edition that helped me to improve the English edition; he and Klaas Louwsma put me right on exactly the man who closed the University of Franeker/Frentsjer.

Chris Perrins went out of his way to retrieve the data on the size of House Martin colonies under the Oxford bridges over time (he also sent a funny of a half-naked W.B. Alexander crossing a river in search of House Martin nests). Ian Newton gave all kinds of feedback, and so did Nicola Crockford. Pete Potts, with the help of Graham Roberts, Richard Levett, David Ball and Chris Webb, assembled unpublished knowledge on the disappearance of House Martins from Selborne and other sites in Hampshire. Rob Fuller helped with the interpretation of the maps in the latest Bird Atlas, and introduced me to BTO as a potential publisher. Les Underhill answered a query about the nesting of House Martins in southern Africa by return of mail.

I have had the pleasure of working together with soul mates and fellow book-lovers like Steven Sterk, Robert Seton, and Barbara Jonkers. Without Steven's motivating way of 'coaching,' this book would not have seen the light of day. I am grateful to Jeff Baker of the British Trust for Ornithology to take this book on board and all his good care. My mother read first drafts in Frisian and provided useful feedback. Abe de Vries edited the Frisian version with a stern pen. René de Vos – who loves the martins and also lives in Gaast – made the translation into Dutch (and contributed a tragic swallow anecdote as he went along), whereas Heidi Disler, with help from her daughter Martine van den Heuvel, produced a first translation into English. In his role as an editor, David Cromack graciously provided the finishing touches to a subsequently expanded text. John Marchant edited and corrected the final manuscript. Jos Zwarts designed the vignettes, and Dick Visser crafted the map illustrating the deep historical connections between the two sides of Mare Frisicum. I was delighted when I discovered that Carry Akroyd would provide the cover artwork!

I was able to write this story because Petra allowed me the space to do so. And although I worked on this book in holiday time, I'd like to thank my employers on Texel (NIOZ Royal Netherlands Institute for Sea Research) and in Groningen (University of Groningen). It is a great privilege to work as a research biologist for these 'old' and fine institutions; to help solve the occasional mystery, and to create new puzzles.

I feel indebted to people who observed hirundines before me and who have written about them so beautifully: people like E.A. Lind in Finland; David Bryant and Angela Turner in England and Scotland; and Douglas Warrick in the United States of America. The retrieving, reading, and re-reading of these works made the writing of this book a big adventure. All you need to give is time.

House Martins live close to people and, as we have seen, it is very easy to record the presence or absence of their breeding activity. With a bit of patience and determination, by just watching what happens at the nest entrances, everybody should be able to also determine the timing of reproduction. When do they finish the building of new clay nests, when do the martins indicate that they are incubating by several times per hour changing incubation shift, and at which dates do small or big nestlings first appear in the nest opening; and have they left? Are the nests used only once, or is there evidence for second broods? Collected by many people over large areas, such House Martin studies can provide us with exciting geographical patterns and better baselines for the future. The Swiss Ornithological Institute has just completed a countrywide, two-year study, and I am delighted that in 2015 the British Trust for Ornithology launched a new citizen-science project to document the state of House Martins in the UK.

Even though it is completely nonsensical – because our human activities don't matter to them, apart from those instances when we disturb their nests, catch them and ring them – my deepest gratitude goes to the House Martins of Gaast. Most of this book was written during summer days when they were hunting vigorously for the arthropods of the air to feed their young – and themselves. I will never be bored by watching their dancing flights above our garden and by daydreaming about them. Their preet and tseep sounds are part of the bliss of a summer in Gaast.

Published sources of information used

Åkesson, S., R. Klaassen, J. Holmgren, J.W. Fox & A. Hedenström. 2012. Migration routes and strategies in a highly aerial migrant, the Common Swift *Apus apus*, revealed by light-level geolocators. *PLoS ONE* 7 (7): e41195.

Appleton, G. 2012. Swifts start to share their secrets. *BTO News* 229: 16–17.

Ashton, J.C. & D.P. Armstrong. 2002. Facultative prioritization of wing growth in the Welcome Swallow *Hirundo neoxena*. *Ibis* 144: 470–477.

Balmer, D.E., S. Gillings, B.J. Caffrey, R.L. Swann, I.S. Downie & R.J. Fuller. 2013. *Bird Atlas 2007–11: the breeding and wintering birds of Britain and Ireland*. BTO Books, Thetford.

Benton, T.G., D.M. Bryant, L. Cole & H.Q.P. Crick. 2002. Linking agricultural practice to insect and bird populations: a historical study over three decades. *Journal of Applied Ecology* 39: 673-687.

Bijlsma, R. 1980. *De Boomvalk*. Kosmos Vogelmonografieën, Amsterdam.

Bijlsma, R. 2012. *Mijn Roofvogels*. AtlasContact, Amsterdam.

Bijlsma, R.G. 2013. Miljoenen Huiszwaluwen *Delichon urbicum* in Afrika, maar waar? *Vogeljaar* 61: 178–183.

Bijlsma, R.G. & B. van den Brink. 2005. A Barn Swallow *Hirundo rustica* roost under attack: timing and risks in the presence of

African Hobbies *Falco cuvieri*. *Ardea* 93: 37–48.

Bijlsma, R.G., F. Hustings & C.J. Camphuysen. 2001. *Algemene en schaarse vogels van Nederland* (Avifauna van Nederland 2). GMB Uitgeverij/KNNV Uitgeverij, Haarlem/Utrecht.

Birkhead, T., J. Wimpenny & B. Montgomery. 2014. *Ten thousand birds. Ornithology since Darwin.* Princeton University Press, Princeton, NJ.

Blythe, R. 1969 (reprinted 2005). *Akenfield. Portrait of a village.* Penguin Classics, London.

Boersma, P. 2006. *Wurdboek fan de Fryske Taal/Woordenboek der Friese taal 22: stûpert-tinken.* Fryske Akademy, Ljouwert.

Bos, J.F.F.P., A.L. Smit & J.J. Schröder. 2013. Is agricultural intensification in The Netherlands running up to its limits? *NJAS – Wageningen Journal of Life Sciences* 66: 65–73.

Bragg, M. 2003. *The adventure of English, 500 AD to 2000. The biography of a language.* Hodder & Stoughton, London.

Bryant, D.M. 1973. The factors influencing the selection of food by the House Martin (*Delichon urbica* (L.)). *Journal of Animal Ecology* 42: 539–564.

Bryant, D.M. 1975. Breeding biology of House Martins *Delichon urbica* in relation to aerial insect abundance. *Ibis* 117: 180–216.

Bryant, D.M. 1978. Environmental influences on growth and survival of nestling House Martins *Delichon urbica*. *Ibis* 120: 271–283.

Bryant, D.M. 1979. Reproductive costs in the House Martin (*Delichon urbica*). *Journal of Animal Ecology* 48: 655–675.

Bryant, D.M. 1988. Lifetime reproductive success of House Martins. Pp. 173–188 in: T.H. Clutton-Brock (ed.), *Reproductive success. Studies of individual variation in contrasting breeding systems.* University of Chicago Press, Chicago.

Bryant, D.M. & A.K. Turner. 1982. Central place foraging by Swallows (Hirundinidae): the question of load size. *Animal Behaviour* 30: 845–856.

Bryant, D.M. & K.R. Westerterp. 1980. The energy budget of the House Martin (*Delichon urbica*). *Ardea* 68: 91-102.

Bullen, A. 2014. *A souvenir guide to Sutton Hoo, Suffolk*. National Trust, Rotherham.

Capelli, C., N. Redhead, J.K. Abernethy, F. Gratrix, J.F. Wilson, T. Moen, T. Hervig, M. Richards, M.P.H. Stumpf, P.A. Underhill, P. Bradshaw, A. Shaha, M.G. Thomas, N. Bradman & D.B. Goldstein. 2003. A Y chromosome census of the British Isles. *Current Biology* 13: 979-984.

Carmiggelt, A. 2000. *De 'Koningsterp' van Wijnaldum. De Friese elite in de vroege Middeleeuwen*. Uitgeverij Uniepers, Abcoude.

Caro, T., K. Beeman, T. Stankovich & H. Whitehead. 2011. The functional significance of coloration in cetaceans. *Evolutionary Ecology* 25: 1231-1245.

Carson, R. 1962. *Silent spring*. Houghton Mifflin, Boston.

Chagnon, M., D. Kreutzweiser, E.A.D. Mitchell, C.A. Morrissey, D.A. Noome & J.P. van der Sluijs. 2014. Risks of large-scale use of systemic insecticides to ecosystem functioning and services. *Environmental Science Pollution Research* 22:119-134

Clare, H. 2009. *Single Swallow: Following an epic journey from South Africa to south Wales*. Chatto & Windus, London.

Deen, M. 2013. *De Wadden. Een geschiedenis*. Thomas Rap, Amsterdam.

Diamond, J. 2001. Deaths of languages. *Natural History* 110 (4): 32-38.

Dokter, A.M., S. Åkesson, H. Beekhuis, W. Bouten, L. Buurma, H. van Gasteren & I. Holleman. 2013. Twilight ascents by common Swifts *Apus apus*, at dawn and dusk: acquisition of orientation cues? *Animal Behaviour* 85: 548-552.

Dykstra, W. 1895. *Uit Friesland's Volksleven van Vroeger en Later: Volksoverleveringen, Volksgebruiken, Volksvertellingen, Volksbegrippen*. M.A. van Seijen, Ljouwert.

Evans, G.E. 1971. *The pattern under the plough. Aspects of the folk-life of East Anglia*. Faber & Faber, London.

Fleming, R. 2011. *Britain after Rome. The fall and rise, 400–1070.* Penguin Books, London.

Gibson, G. 2005. *The bedside book of birds: an avian miscellany.* Bloomsbury, London.

Gill, R.J., O. Ramos-Rodriguez & N.E. Raine. 2012. Combined pesticide exposure severely affects individual- and colony-level traits in bees. *Nature* 491: 105–108.

Goulson, D. 2013. An overview of the environmental risks posed by neonicotinoid insecticides. *Journal of Applied Ecology* 50: 977–987.

Goulson, D. 2013. *A sting in the tale. My adventures with bumblebees.* Jonathan Cape, London.

Goulson, D. 2014. *A buzz in the meadow.* Jonathan Cape, London.

Groen, N.M., R. Kentie, P. de Goeij, B. Verheijen, J.C.E.W. Hooijmeijer & T. Piersma. 2012. A modern landscape ecology of Black-tailed Godwits: habitat selection in southwest Friesland, The Netherlands. *Ardea* 100: 19–28.

Grüebler, M.U., M. Morand & B. Naef-Daenzer. 2008. A predictive model of the density of airborne insects in agricultural environments. *Agriculture, Ecosystems and Environment* 123: 75–80.

Hallmann, C.A., R.P.B. Foppen, C.A.M. van Turnhout, H. de Kroon & E. Jongejans. 2014. Declines in insectivorous birds are associated with high neonicotinoid concentrations. *Nature* 511: 341–343.

Hammers, M., N. von Engelhardt, N.E. Langmore, J. Komdeur, S.C. Griffith & M.J.L. Magrath. 2009. Mate-guarding intensity increases with breeding synchrony in the colonial Fairy Martin, *Petrochelidon ariel. Animal Behaviour* 78: 661–669.

Härke, H. 2011. Anglo-Saxon immigration and ethnogenesis. *Medieval Archaeology* 55: 1–28.

Henry, H., M. Béguin, F. Requier, O. Rollin, J.-F. Odoux, P. Aupinel, J. Aptel, S. Tchamitchian & A. Decourtye. 2012. A common pesticide decreases foraging success and survival in honey bees. *Science* 336: 348–350.

Hill, L.A. 1997. Trans-Sahara recoveries of House Martins *Delichon urbica*, with discussion on ringing, roosting and sightings in Africa. *Safring News* 26: 7–12.
Hills, C. 2003. *Origins of the English*. Duckworth, London.
Hobson, K.A., S.L. Van Wilgenburg, T. Piersma & L.I. Wassenaar. 2012. Solving a migration riddle using isoscapes: House Martins from a Dutch village winter over West Africa. *PLoS ONE 7* (9): e45005.
Hund, K. & R. Prinzinger. 1979. Untersuchungen zur Ortstreue, Paartreue und Überlebensrate nestjunger Vögel bei der Mehlschwalbe *Delichon urbica* in Oberschwaben. *Vogelwarte* 30: 107–117.
Huxley, J.S. 1930. *Bird-watching and bird behaviour*. Chatto and Windus, London.
Jameson, C.M. 2012. *Silent spring revisited*. Bloomsbury, London.
Jonkers, D.A. & H.N. Leys. 1997. Resultaten van de huiszwaluwkolonietellingen in 1996. *Vogeljaar* 45: 167–170.
Jonkman, R.J. & A.P. Versloot. 2008. *Tusken talen. It ferhaal fan de Fryske taal*. Utjouwery Fryslân, Ljouwert.
Jukema, J., Piersma, T., Hulscher, J.B., Bunskoeke, E.J., Koolhaas, A. & Veenstra, A. 2001. *Goudplevieren en wilsterflappers: eeuwenoude fascinatie voor trekvogels*. Ljouwert/Utrecht: Fryske Akademy/KNNV Uitgeverij.
Kentie, R., J.C.E.W. Hooijmeijer, K.B. Trimbos, N.M. Groen & T. Piersma. 2013. Intensified agricultural use of grasslands reduces growth and survival of precocial shorebird chicks. *Journal of Applied Ecology* 50: 243–251.
Klaassen, R., H. Klaassen, A. Berghuis, M. Berghuis, K. Schreven, Y. van der Horst, H. Verkade & L. Kearsley. 2014. Trekroutes en overwinteringsgebieden van Nederlandse Gierzwaluwen ontrafelt met behulp van geolocators. *Limosa* 88: 173–181.
Kožená, I. 1983. Comparison of the diets of young Swallows (*Hirundo rustica*) and House Martins (*Delichon urbica*). *Folia Zoologica* 32: 41–50.

Lack, D. 1956. *Swifts in a tower*. Chapman and Hall, London.
Lagerlöf, S. 1913. *Niels Holgerssons wonderbare reis*. Tweede druk. H.W.J. Becht, Amsterdam.
Lemaire, T. 2007. *Op de vleugels van de ziel. Vogels in voorstelling en verbeelding*. Ambo, Amsterdam.
Lifjeld, J.T. & B. Marstein. 1994. Paternity assurance behaviour in the House Martin *Delichon urbica*. *Journal of Avian Biology* 25: 231–238.
Lind, E.A. 1960. Zur Ethologie und Ökologie der Mehlschwalbe, *Delichon u. urbica* (L.). *Annales Zoologici Societatis 'Vanamo'* 21 (2): 1–123.
Marzal, A., S. Bensch, M. Reviriego, J. Balbontin & F. de Lope. 2008. Effects of malaria double infection in birds: one plus one is not two. *Journal of Evolutionary Biology* 21: 979–987.
Mayr, E. & J. Bond. 1943. Notes on the generic classification of the swallows, Hirundinidae. *Ibis* 85: 334–341.
McCarthy, M. 2014. Immortalised by Macbeth, House Martins thrive in Scotland – but not England. *The Independent*, 10 August 2014: 3.
Mead, C. 2000. *The state of the nations' birds*. Whittet Books, Suffolk.
Menzel, H. 1996. *Die Mehlschwalbe*. Die Neue Brehm-Bücherei Band 548. Spektrum Akademischer Verlag, Heidelberg.
Møller, A.P. 1987. Nest lining in relation to the nesting cycle in the Swallow *Hirundo rustica*. *Ornis Scandinavica* 18: 148–149.
Mynott, J. 2009. *Birdscapes. Birds in our imagination and experience*. Princeton University Press, Princeton.
Nebel, S., A. Mills, J.D. McCracken & P.D. Taylor. 2010. Declines of aerial insectivores in North America follow a geographic gradient. *Avian Conservation and Ecology* 5 (2): 1 [online].
Newton, I. 2004. The recent declines of farmland bird populations in Britain: an appraisal of causal factors and conservation actions. *Ibis* 146: 579–600.
Newton, S. 2003. *The reckoning of King Rædwald. The story of the King linked to the Sutton Hoo ship-burial*. Red Bird Press, Colchester.

Peralta-Sanchez, J.M., A.P. Møller, A.M. Martin-Platero & J.J. Soler. 2010. Number and colour composition of nest lining feathers predict eggshell bacterial community in Barn Swallow nests: an experimental study. *Functional Ecology* 24: 426–433.

Piersma, T. 2008. Female House Martin *Delichon urbica* provisions chicks at nests in two separate subcolonies. *Ardea* 96: 140-144.

Piersma, T. 2013. Timing, nest site selection and multiple breeding in House Martins: age-related variation and the preference for self-built mud nests. *Ardea* 101: 23-32.

Piersma, T. & M. van der Velde. 2009. Breeding season-specific sex diagnostics in the monomorphic House Martin *Delichon urbicum*. *Bird Study* 56: 127-131.

Piersma, T. & M. van der Velde. 2012. Dutch House Martins *Delichon urbicum* gain blood parasite infections over their lifetime, but do not seem to suffer. *Journal of Ornithology* 153: 907–912.

Poortinga, Y. 1976. *De ring fan it ljocht*. Fryske folksforhalen. Bosch & Keuning, Baarn/De Tille, Ljouwert.

Poortinga, Y. 1977. *It fleanend skip. Folksforhalen fan Steven de Bruin*. Bosch & Keuning, Baarn/De Tille, Ljouwert.

Poulin, B., G. Lefebvre & L. Paz. 2010. Red flag for green spray: adverse trophic effects of *Bti* on breeding birds. *Journal of Applied Ecology* 47: 884–889.

Prinzinger, R. & K. Siedle. 1988. Ontogeny of metabolism, thermoregulation and torpor of the House Martin *Delichon u. urbica* (L.) and its ecological significance. *Oecologia* 76: 307–312.

Probst, R., H.L. Nemeschkal, M. McGrady, M. Tucakov & T. Szép. 2011. Aerial hunting techniques and predation success of Hobbies *Falco subbuteo* on Sand Martin *Riparia riparia* at breeding colonies. *Ardea* 99: 9–16.

Radford, M.C. 1966. *The birds of Berkshire and Oxfordshire*. Longmans, Oxford.

Rheinwald, G. 1975. The pattern of settling distances in a population of House Martins *Delichon urbica*. *Ardea* 63: 136–145.

Robinson, R.A., D.E. Balmer & J.H. Marchant. 2008. Survival rates of hirundines in relation to British and African rainfall. *Ringing & Migration* 24: 1–6.

Rowland, H.M. 2009. From Abbott Thayer to the present day: what have we learned about the function of countershading? *Philosophical Transactions of the Royal Society B* 364: 519–527.

Scarfe, N. 1988. *In praise of Suffolk*. Alastair Press, Bury St Edmunds.

Schekkerman, H. & A.J. Beintema. 2007. Abundance of invertebrates and foraging success of Black-tailed Godwit *Limosa limosa* chicks in relation to agricultural grassland management. *Ardea* 95: 39–54.

Sheldon, F.H., L.A. Whittingham, R.G. Moyle, B. Slikas & D.W. Winkler. 2005. Phylogeny of swallows (Aves: Hirundinidae) estimated from nuclear and mitochondrial DNA sequences. *Molecular Phylogenetics and Evolution* 35: 254–270.

Shortall, C.R., A. Moore, E. Smith, M.J. Hall, I.P. Woiwod & R. Harrington. 2009. Long-term changes in the abundance of flying insects. *Insect Conservation and Diversity* 2: 251–260.

Spaar, R., S. Michler, N. Apolloni, J. Hoffmann & S. Rüesch. 2015. A citizen science census of House Martins *Delichon urbicum* in Switzerland led to rethinking conservation strategy (Michler *et al* 2015) [online].

Speerstra, H. 2005. *Cruel Paradise. Life Stories of Dutch Emigrants*. Translated by H.J. Baron. William B. Eerdmans Publishing Company, Grand Rapids, Michigan.

Stenton, F.M. 1971. *Anglo-Saxon England*. Third edition. Oxford University Press, Oxford.

Stokke, B.G., A.P. Møller, B.-E. Sæther, G. Rheinwald & H. Gutscher. 2005. Weather in the breeding area and during migration affects the demography of a small long-distance passerine migrant. *Auk* 122: 637–647.

Strandberg, R., R.H.G. Klaassen, M. Hake, P. Olofsson & T. Alerstam. 2009. Converging migration routes of Eurasian Hobbies *Falco subbuteo*

crossing the African equatorial rain forest. *Proceedings of the Royal Society B* 276: 727–733.
Summers, R.W. 1975. On the ecology of *Crataerina hirundinis* (Diptera: Hippoboscidae) in Scotland. *Journal of Zoology* 175: 557–570.
't Hart, M. 1973. *Ratten*. Arbeiderspers, Amsterdam.
Thomas, M.G., M.P.H. Stumpf & H. Härke. 2008. Integration versus apartheid in post-Roman Britain: a response to Pattison. *Proceedings of the Royal Society B* 275: 2419–2421.
Tscharntke, T., A.M. Klein, A. Kruess, I. Steffan-Dewenter & C. Thies. 2005. Landscape perspectives on agricultural intensification and biodiversity–ecosystem service management. *Ecology Letters* 8: 857–874.
Turner, A.K. 2004. Family Hirundinidae (swallows and martins). Pp. 602–685 in: J. del Hoyo, A. Elliott & D.A. Christie (ed.), *Handbook of the birds of the world*. Vol. 9. Cotingas to pipits and wagtails. Lynx Edicions, Barcelona.
Turner, A. & C. Rose. 1989. *A Handbook to the Swallows and Martins of the World*. Christopher Helm, London.
Twerda, H. 1968. *Fan Fryslâns forline. Fortelboek foar it Fryske folk*. A.J. Osinga, Boalsert.
van de Klundert, B. 2012. *Expeditie Wildernis. Ervaringen met het sublieme in de Nederlandse natuur*. KNNV Uitgeverij/Uitgeverij Landwerk, Zeist.
van der Veen, K.F. 1997. *Wurdboek fan de Fryske Taal/Woordenboek der Friese taal 14: mudde-oansnije*. Fryske Akademy, Ljouwert.
van Ommen, E. & W. Brinkhof. 2006. *De zwaluwen van Singraven*. KNNV Uitgeverij, Utrecht.
Van Reybrouck, D. 2010. *Congo, een geschiedenis*. De Bezige Bij, Amsterdam.
Vickery, J.A., J.R. Tallowin, R.E. Feber, E.J. Asteraki, P.W. Atkinson, R.J. Fuller & V.K. Brown. 2001. The management of lowland neutral grasslands in Britain: effects of agricultural practices on birds and their food resources. *Journal of Applied Ecology* 38: 647–664.

Voipio, P. 1970. On "thunder-flights" of the House Martin *Delichon urbica*. *Ornis Fennica* 47: 15–19.

Von Gunten, K. 1961. Zur Ernährungsbiologie der Mehlschwalbe, *Delichon urbica*: die qualitative Zusammensatzung der Nahrung. *Ornithologische Beobachter* 58: 13–34.

Walker, M.D. & I.D. Rotherham. 2011. No effect of the ectoparasite *Crataerina pallida* on reproduction of Common Swifts *Apus apus*. *Ibis* 153: 416–420.

Warrick, D.R. 1998. The turning- and linear-maneuvering performance of birds: the cost of efficiency for coursing insectivores. *Canadian Journal of Zoology* 76: 1063–1079.

Waugh, D.R. 1978. *Predation strategies in aerial feeding birds*. PhD thesis, University of Stirling.

Weale, M.E., D.A. Weiss, R.F. Jager, N. Bradman & M.G. Thomas. 2002. Y chromosome evidence for Anglo-Saxon mass migration. *Molecular Biology and Evolution* 19: 1008–1021.

Westell, W.P. 1910. *British nesting birds. A complete record of every species which nests in the British Isles*. J.M. Dent, London.

White, G. 1788–1789 (reprinted 1977). *The natural history of Selborne*. Penguin Books, Harmondsworth.

Whitehorn, P.R., S. O'Connor, F.L. Wackers & D. Goulson. 2012. Neonicotinoid pesticide reduces bumble bee colony growth and queen production. *Science* 336: 351–352.

Whittingham, L.A. & J.T. Lifjeld. 1995. Extra-pair fertilizations increase the opportunity for sexual selection in the monogamous House Martin *Delichon urbica*. *Journal of Avian Biology* 26: 283–288.

Winkler, D.W. 1993. Use and importance of feathers as nest lining in Tree Swallows (*Tachycineta bicolor*). *Auk* 110: 29–36.

Winkler, D.W. 2006. Roosts and migrations of Swallows. *El Hornero* 21: 85–97.

Winkler, D.W. & F.H. Sheldon. 1993. Evolution of nest construction in swallows (Hirundinidae): a molecular phylogenetic perspective. *Proceedings of the National Academy of Sciences* 90: 5705–5707.

Wojciechowski, M.S. & R. Yosef. 2011. House Martins respond to perceived danger. *Journal of Ethology* 29: 93–97.

Woodward, I. 2014. House Martins. Field testing for a 2015 survey. *Bird Table*, 79: 14-16.

Woodward, I. & D. Balmer. 2014. A new survey, in black & white. *BTO News* 312: 8–9.

Wright, J., S. Markman & S.M. Denney. 2006. Facultative adjustment of pre-fledging mass loss by nestling Swifts preparing for flight. *Proceedings of the Royal Society B* 273: 1895–1900.

Theunis Piersma, an animal ecologist at the University of Groningen and the NIOZ Royal Netherlands Institute for Sea Research, is passionate about sharing the stories of the birds that he studies with his team. Currently the Chair in Flyway Ecology, he tries to shape the best possible ecological research on migrant birds in wetland habitats. A contributor to over 400 scientific publications, and within strong international collaborations, he focuses on individual animals, with deep consideration of their environmental context. He is the founder of the applied research consortium Global Flyway Network, and co-authored the enthusiastically received *The flexible phenotype. A body-centred integration of ecology, physiology, and behaviour* (Oxford University Press, 2011). In 2014 Theunis received the prestigious Spinoza Premium, the highest accolade for working scientists in the Netherlands.